LEVEL THE CURVE

Oliver Gelles &
Dr. Jamie Reynolds

LEVEL
THE
CURVE

Data-Driven Practice Management
Principles to Compete in Today's Changing
Orthodontic Landscape

 | Books

Published by Advantage, Charleston, South Carolina.
Member of Advantage Media.

ADVANTAGE is a registered trademark, and the Advantage colophon is a trademark of Advantage Media Group, Inc.

Printed in the United States of America.

10 9 8 7 6 5 4 3 2 1

ISBN: 978-1-64225-643-7 (Paperback)
ISBN:978-1-64225-642-0 (eBook)

LCCN: 2023906493

Cover design by Megan Elger.
Layout design by Matthew Morse.

Advantage Media helps busy entrepreneurs, CEOs, and leaders write and publish a book to grow their business and become the authority in their field. Advantage authors comprise an exclusive community of industry professionals, idea-makers, and thought leaders. Do you have a book idea or manuscript for consideration? We would love to hear from you at **AdvantageMedia.com.**

For Walker, Dante, Reese, and Caden

*Special thanks also to Koz and Dave for all their hard work,
leadership, mentorship, and expertise*

CONTENTS

PART I
CREATING THE VALUE PROPOSITION

PART II
INTELLIGENT FLEXIBILITY

PART III
CONVERSION DEEP DIVE

INTRODUCTION

Whoever desires constant success must change
his or her conduct with the times.

—NICCOLO MACHIAVELLI

Every kind of innovation begins with a problem that needs to be solved, and my own particular dilemma as an orthodontist was trying to practice orthodontics in Detroit during the Great Recession of 2007–2009, after paying a premium at the height of the economy to begin buying into a practice. What you may not know is that when the recession hit the rest of the country, Detroit was just beginning its slow recovery. That involved a complete reimagining of the "Big Three" US automakers—General Motors, Ford, and Chrysler—and a renegotiating of their union contracts. Many in Detroit had already lost their jobs and begun their exodus from the city even before the recession started to impact the rest of the country. When the banking crisis emerged, and the US economy began to spiral, Detroit saw some of the worst of it—after already experiencing the automotive-related "prerecession." Those were tough financial times, and they hit my practice hard!

I had no idea what to do. Being a clinical orthodontist at heart, I'd spent the first decade of my career focusing almost exclusively on developing my clinical skills. When sitting for my recertification as a diplomate of the American Board of Orthodontics (ABO), for example, I helped push the envelope in digitally customized treatment by including the first Insignia case submitted for the ABO exam. But that clinical expertise didn't help me when the recession struck. Along with others in my specialty, I watched my practice experience a steep drop in case acceptance and production. I suddenly realized being an accomplished clinician wasn't the only requirement for achieving and sustaining a successful practice.

Since I was already working with Dr. Jeff Kozlowski at the time (and still do), the two of us began "grasping at straws," trying to find some way to help our patients afford quality orthodontic treatment during what were very tough economic times. Aware that new patient starts are the lifeblood of any practice, both Jeff and I (especially I) were confident we could win additional patients by doing better in several key areas of practice management. But we just couldn't identify why we were subpar in those areas or, most importantly, how to improve. To make matters worse, Jeff had been following the dictates of a leading practice-management consultant who ruled his financial flexibility with a proverbial iron fist. It was obvious we needed a fresh approach. So we started seeking help from people with business expertise outside orthodontic practice.

We were fortunate to have Dave Ternan—a business consultant with broad experience in large companies and start-ups—help us evaluate the foundational principles driving our practice management. It turned out we'd been relying on too many outdated industry practices, myths, and assumptions that were largely based on complacency, convention, or the dreaded "That is how we have always done it." As we dug deeper still, we discovered a lot of these old orthodontic standards were actually hurting, not helping, our practices. It was obvious we'd have to implement some serious changes before our misdirected methods ruined all chance of recovery. That prospect was all too real since Detroit's economic crisis had already forced several orthodontic offices in our immediate area to close permanently.

In a last-ditch attempt to survive, we went on a kind of myth-busting quest, using our practices as guinea pigs to collect and examine data that showed which business ideas worked and which didn't. Once we had changed course, we had not only adapted to the downturn successfully, but we'd actually come out stronger. Although Detroit (and our practice) had been hard hit economically, our business struggles actually turned out to be a blessing in disguise since they had exposed the outmoded or insufficient ideas or processes we had in place in our practice. But discarding counterproductive ideas and methods was just the beginning of our business transformation.

As Jeff Kozlowski, Dave Ternan, and I watched the landscape of orthodontics evolve after the recession, we witnessed some practices enjoy wild success, while others failed. Determined to gain a deeper understanding of why, as well as create a potential solution, we decided to compare their business models to our own. We asked a group of colleagues and like-minded orthodontists who also ran successful practices, then mixed in "real" businesspeople and tasked them with the mission of finding the optimal way to operate a practice. Doing so prompted Jeff and I, along with Dave Ternan and many of the doctors we had collaborated with, to create OrthoFi—the software and service solution we used to find data-driven novel or improved ways to approach the business side of our practices. (Disclosure: as of the writing of this book, we each own shares of OrthoFi stock.)

A Better Way Forward

Since creating our software solution, we have used it to assess large data sets collected from over one million patient starts and over $5 billion in orthodontic production. Those numbers enabled us to zero in on the most effective method for running a successful practice and eliminate the guesswork from practice management. By collaboratively simplifying our numbers-driven methodology, we discovered what worked and what didn't in terms of practice management. Our results verified that we'd been right to question the antiquated ways of our profession and proved that applying the new gold standards we'd codified worked. It was a watershed Mom:ent for us, as we realized orthodontists would no longer have to resort to the costly "trial and error" method of the past. For the first time, doctors could rely on a data-proven methodology rather than opinion, conjecture, or gut feelings. Our innovative software had succeeded in facilitating a better way of operating—one encompassing a unique, data-driven philosophy of payment flexibility, based on a core understanding of collections, delinquency, and the benefits of outsourcing.

Provided in this book is data drawn from the hundreds of practices representing hundreds of thousands of patients and billions in orthodontic production. Coauthored with industry strategist and marketing leader Oliver Gelles, our book contains information drawn from the largest and cleanest data set on consumer buying habits ever collected in the orthodontic, and likely any elective healthcare, space.

Together, we've studied, refined, created, and promoted the global adoption of data analytics and technological innovation within our industry. As part of that effort, we've written this book to share essential best practices and to advocate for what we call the "new gold standards" that Dave Ternan and Jeff Kozlowski (and many others) helped develop and test in orthodontic practices all over the country—standards that have been wildly successful for practice profitability and improved patient service. But before Oliver and I share those gold standards, you need to know which ones we've abandoned—and why we discarded them.

Outdated Orthodontic Standards

Which of the widely accepted orthodontic business practices are counterproductive? Since there are quite a few of them, we'll cover the many we've identified throughout the coming chapters of this book. We will spotlight three of the most important outdated practices you'll need to immediately discard to become more profitable. These old standards are hurting not only your bottom line but your patients as well.

1. A Patient's Payment Window Must Match Their Treatment Time

Our recommendation to stop restricting a patient's payment window to the length of their treatment initially turned heads, but it's likely the major barrier to your practice's growth. Traditional financing methodologies dictate tying a patient's financing plans to their estimated treatment time and then not removing the braces until they were paid due to fear they would stop paying after debond. We used to question that, too, and we realize it goes

THESE OLD STANDARDS ARE HURTING NOT ONLY YOUR BOTTOM LINE BUT YOUR PATIENTS AS WELL.

against conventional thinking. But the data from hundreds of thousands of payment plans simply doesn't support that position. Despite what you may think, delinquency rates in our industry are already extremely low—around 3 percent past due beyond thirty days.

And the majority of delinquency happens long before treatment term (much more on this later).

2. Collection Processes Need to Be Onerous to Be Effective

Many orthodontists still believe aggressive collection procedures are a necessary evil, but the data shows they aren't necessary. Instead, we now know collections should be handled just like every other aspect of clinic planning—systematically and consistently, with the end in mind. Patients who owe money are far more likely to cooperate if they feel they're being respected rather than hounded. Our data shows only an average of 1 percent active patient receivables past due beyond thirty days. This is far below the national average of 3 percent,* and that equates to significant improvements in collections, cash flow, and ultimately, the bottom line—while still offering every patient flexible payment terms.

3. You Have to Cover Costs on Every Case by Getting 15 to 20 Percent Up Front Every Time

OK, let's talk down payments. For the longest time, practices have mandated that it's essential to cover up-front clinical costs by getting 15 to 20 percent of the total fee before starting treatment. You may be wondering why that isn't relevant anymore, but honestly we're not sure it was ever relevant; it's just what orthodontists normally did. But patients are also consumers, and consumers now expect (and need) payment customization as never before. So even though requiring a specific down payment before starting treatment is the way doctors have conducted business for decades, it doesn't work well in today's increasingly competitive and consumer-driven business environment.

Although it's been well documented by the Federal Reserve that 37 percent of consumers don't have the discretionary funds to even cover small, unexpected expenses of $400, many ask patients to pay at least $1,500 down to start with aligners or other popular high-tech treatments. Unfortunately, this sum can be a huge obstacle to a lot of families and is likely killing your conversion. Especially for adults, whose consumer behavior is much more whimsical and spontaneous. This scenario poses a double challenge for orthodontists wanting to treat additional patients while also protecting their practice's cash flow with down payments that cover lab expenses.

Historically, most doctors were trained to think in a transactional way: to focus on each individual payment plan and evaluate the performance of that plan in a vacuum. But we suggest a better way—the one preferred by traditional financial institutions that use a broader, more aggregated blended method of evaluating performance—based on cohorts rather than individuals. So if you're willing to set aside the fear of change and outdated practice-management dogma, we'll show you how expanding your payment options will actually protect, and even increase, your cash flow better than the old transactional payment concept our profession has relied on for so long. Key to our approach is a proven concept we call "open choice," which utilizes patient-customized payment options instead.

Success by the Numbers

Orthodontists spend ten or eleven years preparing for their specialization, but they often get little or no business-management training before they start offering services to patients. At best, they may receive on-the-job training from the senior doctor who likely learned their business practices from the doctor preceding them. That means the vast majority of orthodontists simply aren't aware of the way this gap in their knowledge base can limit, or even damage, their practices—which is why we have been sharing data analytics in blogs, articles, and lectures for years and why we consolidated the end-to-end philosophy in this book. By providing the business solutions you'll need to succeed in what is now a very different industry, we'll show you how to engage your patients and team to drive growth.

Creating a reliable business-management approach for the evolving industry of orthodontics wasn't easy. Doing so required first gaining a comprehensive understanding of the specialty's current status and how it's being impacted by new technology and changing consumer trends. Fortunately, the digital age in dentistry made that quantifiable for the first time by providing the massive amount of raw data OrthoFi and OrthoBanc were able to parse and interpret with advanced statistics and business analytics. Our analysis has enabled us to assemble the data-driven tools, techniques, and procedures that solve common practice problems while simplifying the complex business-management aspects of your practice. The result is a better-run office that benefits your patients and at the same time grows your business. That, of course, is a win-win for everyone, and it's the path to orthodontic business growth at a time when the old industry rules no longer apply.

Our Changing Industry

As the orthodontic industry grows more competitive, any discussion of practice standards needs to emphasize that the integrity of your clinical practice and decision-making must be unimpeachable. You should never make decisions for any reason other than your truest clinical judgment, and you must treat every patient with the same treatment plans you would suggest for a family member. Industry sources indicate the average orthodontic practice adhering to that high standard still grows 2.5 to 4 percent annually, enjoys excellent cash flow, and has very low default risk compared to just about any other industry. In addition, practices typically see excellent performance across the board with 35 to 55 percent profit margins.

Those statistics are certainly reassuring, but you may be surprised to find out they actually disguise the greatest threat our industry faces today—and, no, that threat isn't the competition of direct-to-consumer (DTC) orthodontics, the question of whether Align needs doctors to operate, DSOs, or even the dentist up the road doing orthodontic work. The danger is actually posed by the very ease with which most later- and middle-career doctors have achieved their success. In the past, a successful practice was nearly guaranteed in an industry that only had about nine thousand specialists servicing the orthodontic needs of over three hundred million patients. Historically, that happy scenario meant that succeeding as an orthodontist was as simple as catching crooked-teeth fish from a very small barrel, even though many in the profession felt the industry was very competitive. This situation also created a misleading condition we've termed economic confirmation bias: the belief that their financial success validates their existing procedures and strategies—even though it's likely they're doing a number of things wrong. If you suffer from this bias, you probably think, *I make a lot of money, so I must be doing a lot of things right.*

In business, that kind of assumption represents a reactive approach to success that hangs on the knife edge of circumstances. Conditions can change rapidly, and in the orthodontic industry, they already have. The favorable industry dynamics of the past have created a false sense of security that won't protect you from the powerful combination of a new consumer profile and more sophisticated corporate competition. Times have changed for orthodontists, and they will continue to do so. Thanks to an ever-expanding array of technological and philosophical advances in the field of dentistry, your potential patients now have a much wider variety of treatment options. We must adapt to remain the place where orthodontic patients continue to choose to have their orthodontic treatment.

Curbing Economic Confirmation Bias

Like a tsunami you don't see coming until it is too late, economic confirmation bias poses a serious danger to every orthodontist's continued growth and success. If doctors currently have a successful practice, for example, most assume this means they're doing everything right and don't need to change anything for their success to continue unabated. Is that you? Since orthodontists have historically done well financially, relative to other professions, you might think your past (or current) success proves you're on

YOUR TEAM, APTITUDE, SKILL, CLINICAL PASSION, AND EVEN THE IMPACT OF OUTSIDE ECONOMIC FORCES ARE NOT THE REAL PROBLEMS—IT'S A COMPLACENT MINDSET THAT'S THE REAL HAZARD.

point, but that's an incredibly dangerous assumption. When overconfidence is coupled with a radically changing demographic and rapid technological innovation, industry disruption is inevitable. Confirmation bias touches even the most successful companies. Blockbuster signed their death warrant by succumbing to confirmation bias. They were offered the opportunity to invest in an upstart home entertainment company called Netflix. Instead of thinking proactively about how the market and their customers were evolving, they chose to believe that they were big because they were better. They also allowed themselves to be trapped within a prison of their own making. In the end, they declined to invest in streaming technology because it would eliminate late fees, a material source of their revenue at the time. If it can happen to a goliath like Blockbuster, it can happen to you. In fact, it's already happening as you read this. We really can't emphasize this enough. Your team, aptitude, skill, clinical passion, and even the impact of outside economic forces are not the real problems—it's a complacent mindset that's the real hazard.

While doctors are resting on their laurels, savvy corporate players are buying into the industry who aren't constrained by this collectively inherited and reductive mindset. It's best to face facts: this growing host of competitors are armed with serious business skills, a tireless work ethic, deep pockets, and a much better concept of consumer sales and marketing than the vast majority of practicing orthodontists in private practice. Yet this daunting corporate consolidation doesn't have to be the "iocane powder" poison of the private practitioner (that's a movie reference from *The Princess Bride* for those in the cheap seats). The future of elective healthcare is to maintain or improve your clinical skills while also increasing your knowledge of sales and marketing. If you don't, an increasing number of people won't be choosing you as their orthodontic care provider—which isn't typically what's best for patients. Sadly, most patients mistakenly think less-qualified providers represent a positive change for consumers like themselves. They simply don't know any better and welcome what seems to be extraconvenient or affordable options to improve their dental health and their smiles.

In this changing practice environment, you'll have to learn new business and leadership skills you were never taught during residency—skills that don't come naturally to the majority of doctors—if you want to preserve and grow the value of your practice. You'll need to switch away from the old orthodontic standards you've been using and build your practice back up with the new gold standards your competition is probably already using. Because no practice demographic is identical, the approach we recommend should be customized by data that pinpoints how to best serve the ideal patients in your area. In the chapters ahead, we're going to break that down into incremental steps you can start applying right away. After all, improving your business acumen is in the best interest of your new and existing patients, who deserve to be treated by a highly trained orthodontist.

What You'll Find in the Chapters Ahead

Orthodontists are facing new challenges in a rapidly changing industry that's growing more competitive by the day. So it's time to leave your confirmation bias behind and learn how to outperform your competitors by serving your patients better than they can. Although the rising competition may look daunting to those with a conventional practice, there's no need to panic! This book not only describes the correct strategic response but also explains how to start implementing that strategy right away. It's a powerful business development tool for the orthodontist who wants to optimize the success of their services and practices in an evolving industry landscape. In the following pages, we not only identify the key changes that practices and providers need to act upon, but we also break those changes down into incremental, actionable steps and describe the latest and best tools you'll want to start using immediately. Those who own their own practices, or eventually plan to, will find this book most valuable, but orthodontists everywhere will discover it facilitates increased success in their profession overall. That's because an understanding of the business principles and strategies inside these pages will make any orthodontic doctor a greater asset to their practice or employer.

In the sections and chapters that follow, we provide the essential business advice and proven, data-driven concepts you'll need to help improve both the value and profitability of your services and practices. With those two objectives in mind, this book's three sections are ordered to provide a sequential, reliable road map to your business's growth and success. First, we make the case for how you can create optimal value for your patients. Second, we list the steps needed to improve your back office. Third, we take a deeper dive into the concepts behind those steps to show you how and why they work—concepts supported by data we'll share to prove what actually works and what doesn't.

Our purpose in doing so is to arm orthodontic doctors like you with the knowledge to grow and thrive, despite the ominous industry trends that are already impacting your new patient starts. We'll present a system that can transform a practice from good to great by showing you how to work smarter, not harder. That way, you can focus on driving growth in your business while deriving greater enjoyment from doing what you do best. But most importantly, you'll be able to better serve your patients by learning and implementing the following aspects of our system:

- Procedures to boost starts by creating flexibility, generating higher conversion
- Techniques that use leverage and open choice to maximize growth, stabilize cash flow, and manage default risk
- Methods for managing follow-ups that stop "leaks in the bucket"
- Routines that implement better back-office systems

Here's the Bottom Line

You're incredibly busy, and you don't have time to wade through business-management theory to figure out what will work to grow your practice as you strive to create added value for your patients. So we've done that work for you by giving you actionable metrics, fueled by big data, that are directly relevant to orthodontists. To that end, we've harvested information gleaned from the leading-edge digital tools, services, and appliances doctors are now using, drawing from a powerful set of measurements never previously available in the profession. If you're not using these statistical sets to grow the value of your company and services, you're going to get left behind. Every profession is moving toward data-driven analytics and strategies because they work better, faster, and more accurately than flying blind or relying on your gut. That's where we come in. This book will share the indispensable stats, tools, and techniques required to grow your practice while avoiding costly pitfalls that keep you from serving your patients most effectively.

Part I
CREATING THE VALUE PROPOSITION

Orthodontics has entered a new era, and the old historical model of simply hanging out a shingle touting the title "orthodontist" is no longer enough to bring people into your practice. In the current business environment, it's crucial to focus on learning how to create and deliver value in a way that gives your patients, your office teams, and the industry itself what they actually want and need. To achieve both, you must understand and respond to the market trends showing what patients want most in an orthodontic provider. This kind of evidence-based analysis will enable you to engage your patients and your teams in the meaningful way needed to drive healthy practice growth.

Of course, the foundation of such growth in all successful orthodontic practices is using every opportunity to engage and build relationships with new patients. It's only logical that the best way to do so is knowing what those patients want in the first place—before they're seen virtually or in person for the first time. Once a practice is equipped with patient satisfaction data, for example, you can use that feedback to proactively offer new patients value in a way that resonates with them. Instead of blindly guessing market trends, business analytics enables you to "see" the actionable steps you can take to create better value for your patients. It provides the kind of twenty-twenty business vision you'll need to remain competitive. Knowing and acting upon these indicators will be your best guide to optimizing your efforts, enabling you to work smarter, instead of harder. In this section of the book, we'll also show you why and how you need to change the lens through which you assess your practice performance so you can improve it.

1

VALUE FOR YOUR PATIENTS/CUSTOMERS

The customer tells us how to stay in business,
[so it's] best that we listen.

— PAMELA NELSON, PRESIDENT AND CEO,
BRACANE RESEARCH COMPANY

Through new patient intake surveys, patients have told us what they value in orthodontic treatment are quality, comfort, technology, and affordability. When surveyed, patients made it crystal clear those four factors were most important to them. Patients also responded that they really value easy and convenient treatment—something we'll talk more about shortly. This being the case, it's only logical that the first step to making your orthodontic services appealing is to create value for patients by offering what they've already indicated they actually want. You can be as flexible as you like with payment options, but if you've got a practice that doesn't successfully address the needs and desires of your patients (like your competitors), fewer and fewer prospective patients will opt to pay your fees, no matter how friendly or affordable you make them.

We used to ponder daily how to help other orthodontists create better messaging for their practices. We eventually realized the first important step was determining what patients actually wanted rather than assuming what we thought they wanted. To figure that out, we designed a novel, slider-based patient questionnaire that patients and parents were asked to fill out as part of their online forms before they were seen for an exam. We asked patients to use slider bars to rank the importance of various orthodontic treatment factors on a scale of 1 to 5, with 1 being "Not important" and 5 being "Extremely important."

Patients were asked to rank the following factors:

- Length (speed) of treatment
- Comfort
- Latest technology
- Clear or invisible technology
- Low down payment
- Low monthly payment
- Quality of treatment
- How interested are you in starting within a month?

Once we'd gathered and analyzed all the questionnaire responses, it was easy to see which items were most popular on patients' "wish lists." These results made it obvious orthodontic practices could be more intentional and proactive about offering patients the value they've been seeking. After pooling and assessing all of our compiled data, we weren't too surprised to find that patients' highest priority was "quality of treatment." Nearly everyone indicated quality was "extremely important" to them, and they consistently ranked it first across the board. The "comfort" factor ranked second, and "latest technology" and "low monthly payment" tied for third place in importance to customers. Those findings told us people want access to high-tech treatment, but they prefer to pay for it with a low monthly payment—a factor that speaks to the issue of affordability versus price. In other words, patients want and need treatment to be affordable more than they need treatment to be less expensive overall.

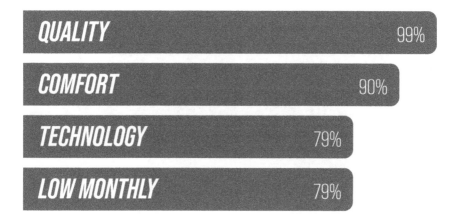

What actionable steps does this information suggest? First and foremost, our data clearly indicates that the services and messaging across your practice must focus on treatment that offers quality, comfort, technology, and affordability since those are the four attributes your patients prioritize. Although every practice needs to create value on a person-by-person basis that considers the wants and needs of each individual, the focus of your overall messaging and services should be centered on offering patients the highest-quality, most comfortable, and most affordable technology possible.

The other thing we found interesting was that one of the least important things to people was clear technology. Only 40 percent ranked "clear/invisible" as important, very important, or extremely important. As expected, the majority of those were adults. And fewer than 20 percent of parents who filled out the questionnaire for their kids ranked clear/invisible as important—which was initially surprising, given the rise in popularity of clear aligners and lingual braces.

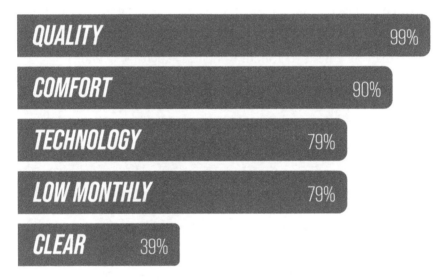

QUALITY	99%
COMFORT	90%
TECHNOLOGY	79%
LOW MONTHLY	79%
CLEAR	39%

Many of you have probably assumed you needed to compete head to head with "clear aligner or bust" messaging that offered clear treatment at a lower price. But our data shows that kind of knee-jerk reaction is actually shortsighted because it doesn't consider the broader market. After analyzing new patient data, for example, we've found the best message for prospective orthodontic patients is that your practice provides higher quality, greater comfort, and the best technology in a way that's more affordable (on a monthly basis). Clear solutions are essential for today's practice. But it's your expertise as an orthodontist, not "clear" technologies, that needs to be the primary focus of your universal marketing appeal.

While it's true that quality and comfort have the broadest appeal across all markets, our survey results also indicate the need to customize your message for each individual when you're in the new patient room presenting treatment. Each person is a distinct individual, and getting to know their unique wants and desires prior to discussing treatment options is going to be key to them choosing your practice. This means gathering meaningful information about your patients' concerns through online forms they submit before you present treatment is a crucial step. Such info provides a kind of "answer key" that allows you to adjust your marketing message for each

IT'S YOUR EXPERTISE AS AN ORTHODONTIST, NOT "CLEAR" TECHNOLOGIES, THAT NEEDS TO BE THE PRIMARY FOCUS OF YOUR UNIVERSAL MARKETING APPEAL.

person and helps ensure that patients and parents leave your new patient room knowing you've customized their treatment plans and resolved any concerns they might have had when they came in. Besides adding value, *the singular goal of every treatment consultation is to identify and address any objections or obstacles the prospective patient may have to following your recommendation to begin orthodontic treatment.* Your specialized expertise makes you the most knowledgeable person to resolve such issues, helping patients understand all the ways that treatment will benefit them—something they simply can't know unless you explain it to them in a way that they understand and value.

Smaller Wait Lists Drive Success

When thinking about the success of your practice, you might be tempted to take pride in the size of your wait list for exams. But is your long wait list helping your ego while hurting your practice? We analyzed that question by evaluating whether there was a point at which waiting for an exam set too far in the future would increase the odds a patient would be more likely to skip their scheduled appointment and go someplace else in the interim. That turned out to be true.

THE SINGULAR GOAL OF EVERY TREATMENT CONSULTATION IS TO IDENTIFY AND ADDRESS ANY OBJECTIONS OR OBSTACLES THE PROSPECTIVE PATIENT MAY HAVE.

When appointments involved children, having to wait longer than three weeks caused their kept exam rates to fall, but the same thing happened with adults after just a few days. Anything longer than that, and the data suggested the odds of a patient keeping their exam fell significantly (which probably means they found a different practice or changed their mind about the urgency of orthodontics). It turns out that convenience often outweighed all other factors. In other words, we found out that what helps the orthodontist's pride (a long wait list) isn't actually adding value for prospective patients who will grow increasingly discontented with every day they're forced to wait for their appointment.

The moral of that business story is clear. When your practice is running with a significant wait list (five to six weeks) for prime-time exam appointments, you should consider one of several options to alleviate pent-up demand:

Option 1. If your exam slots are sixty minutes or longer, consider shortening them to forty-five minutes. Many, many excellent providers utilize a forty-five-minute exam spot. Many use fewer. Any more than forty-five minutes is likely resulting from a bloated exam process. Two possible ways we have seen success in shortening exams are as follows:

    a. Less doctor exams: We typically don't advocate for an exam at which the doctor doesn't see the patient (aka a 'doctorless' exam). In fact, in our practices we mandate the patient see a doctor at each visit. However, training your team to be more skilled in presenting the treatment plan and financials before the doctor enters the room saves time. Almost every doctor includes too much detail in their treatment plan explanations. We can't help ourselves. Let the treatment coordinator present everything, and make yourself available for questions at the end. This is a much more efficient workflow.

b. Emphasize completing the necessary paperwork and insurance information collection *before* the exam arrives. Filling out paperwork that can be done beforehand and waiting for insurance benefits verification and calculation is unnecessary with today's mobile technology. Adopt a software system that lets you do this work ahead of time.

Option 2. If you only have one treatment coordinator (TC), hire and train another one to offer an additional column of exams during the high-demand time slot each day. Even if you lack the volume to devote those appointments entirely to sales, the increased production generated from availability and convenience will overwhelmingly pay for the payroll increase. It may also be necessary to evaluate your exam process to decrease the amount of doctor time requisite in the exam process to allow two TC columns to run effectively in the busiest high-demand hours. When executed properly, you'll find your efforts will be handsomely rewarded.

Option 3. Continue to offer a process that allows virtual evaluations in the post-COVID-19 era. Doing so will permit your TC to schedule consultations with parents in the midmorning at a time when their busy child is in school, and the TC often has open exam slots. Parents usually aren't as busy at this time, but if they are, virtual consultations can easily and quickly be conducted from their workplace, so they can avoid the time-consuming trip into your office.

Option 4. Consider hiring an associate to meet the patient demand represented by your overly long wait list. The additional patients will easily pay for the extra expense of another doctor while making your services most accessible and convenient, something that's increasingly important to today's consumer.

Option 5. Consider adopting remote monitoring technology. These technologies extend your capacity and that of your team by reducing in-office visits, tracking treatment progress, and providing insightful analytics to improve clinical efficiency. This is not advocating for an "all aligner" or "all anything else" practice. Yet even in today's marketplace, there are still practices not using clear aligners, not using digital braces technologies, and not using scanners as the entry points to these treatments. Adopting a more digital-first workflow will allow you to "start" with a scan, which a trained technician can take accurately in five minutes or less, and not with a direct bond procedure, which can take forty-five minutes or more and include the operational challenges with accommodating placing one or two arches of braces on demand.

These actions will not only add value for your patients in terms of convenience and better customer service but will also provide extra revenue opportunities and greater profitability for your practice. If you are going to offer real value to your patients, you will want to ensure you have room for them so you can accommodate them as quickly as possible.

CAPTURING ADULT PATIENTS REQUIRES UNDERSTANDING WHAT THEY VALUE—TIME AND CONVENIENCE.

Adult demand for orthodontic treatment, in particular, is driving a significant amount of growth in the industry, but capturing adult patients requires understanding what they value—time and convenience. Adults seeking treatment for themselves instead of their child will tend to be more spontaneous and "want driven" than "need driven." That means your TC will have to respond quickly if they're going to schedule exams with adults who are often seeking to begin treatment in a spur-of-the-Mom:ent kind of way. What if they call your office during their lunch hour at work? We'll talk about that in a Mom:ent.

Patient Referrals Are Value Driven

In the past, orthodontic practices relied on a steady stream of professional referrals and an occasional patient referral. But times have changed, and the practices of today are now fueled, driven, and sustained by mostly patient-to-patient referrals instead of professional referrals—a reality that's forced those in the industry to view their practice from a completely different perspective. We aren't suggesting you forget about professional relationships and that you shouldn't continue to cultivate the value of your practice to dentists. What we are suggesting is that patient-generated referrals are much more controllable and important for your practice at a time when more orthodontic practices are done by other dental providers or kept in house with multispecialty offices. Patient referrals are the fuel that will drive your practice forward toward steady, sustainable growth. Unfortunately, patient referrals do not rain down in buckets in direct response to successful patient outcomes the way you might wish. To generate these referrals, you'll need to prioritize a few major tenets for your practice:

Your clinical outcomes need to be beyond reproach. When creating value for your patients, it's exquisitely and unquestionably important you treat them with altruistic clinical integrity at all times. This means you never recommend treatment if you wouldn't do so for your own family. That being said, it's also important to remember each of your patients is also a customer with their own set of priorities and goals for their treatment. In short, many of your customers/patients won't necessarily appreciate the medical or technical sophistication of your treatment approach and outcome since they will use their own set of criteria to determine the success of their treatment. To best serve your customers/patients, you'll obviously have to make sure you focus on both what the patient needs (according to the tenets of orthodontic clinical excellence) and what the customer would like as well.

Outcome-based work is a dirty job, but someone has to do it. The medical and technical aspects of orthodontic outcomes usually make providers a lot happier than their patients. Beyond a certain level, patients simply won't notice the subtle improvements you've provided, and it might not drive your practice growth either, even if you've done the absolute best for them clinically. Knowing that, it's best to view your patients through two lenses: (1) as people who need to be treated with clinical integrity, and (2) as customers seeking value in their preferred service style and outcome. In other words, achieving successful outcomes with a patient requires you to increase your focus on their identity as a customer seeking value.

Outcomes don't really create happy patients. Instead, outcomes are a threshold motivator, which means treatment results have to reach a certain level to please patients and to please the dental/referral community as well. Beyond that point, most above-level results are irrelevant to the vast majority of patients. Again, this is not permission or guidance to lower your clinical standards. Do not! Orthodontists must continue to be the gold standard of clinical excellence. But do not rely on your clinical outcomes as the means by which patients will differentiate or value your practice. It is also crucial for us to understand and deliver facial and smile aesthetics in our treatments. Socking in the buccal occlusion is as important as ever for long-term dental health, but nonextraction and facial-appearance-driven treatments are the future of our profession and critical to the continued role of the orthodontist as the elite provider for smile and occlusal results. And elite, aesthetically driven results include becoming excellent in hard and soft tissue contouring as well as offering whitening treatments in office. We need to be the leaders in delivering an amazing smile, not just aligned teeth.

We need to know what our customers want and what they think of us. Successful businesses rely on creating objective measurements of customer satisfaction rather than using "intuition" or some other subjective method. One popular tool is the net promoter score (NPS), which delivers an objective "score" and rating, based on the number of positive and negative responses received on a particular customer survey. On a scale of 1 to 10, the NPS is a measure of your "promoters" and "detractors," giving you an idea of how well your business is perceived. To find out your NPS, for example, you would ask your patients, "How likely are you to refer a friend or colleague to use this business?" The way they answer will tell you how powerfully (or not) patient referrals will be driving your practice's growth.

Only patients responding with a 9 or 10 are considered promoters, indicating they are superhappy with your practice and will be likely to recommend you to someone else. Detractors are those rating your practice with anything from 0 to 6, which means only the happiest of patients are actually going to be a reliable source of referrals. Most of the rest are considered "detractors"—something which may change the lens through which you prioritize your approach to customer service. NPS numbers are incredibly valuable, since they're designed to tell you how healthy your referral pipeline is and how likely people are to refer your business to others.

Unfortunately, the orthodontic industry has not really used the NPS (or any other way) to broadly survey patients, and whatever meager information was collected in the past hasn't been shared within the industry in a meaningful way. To rectify that oversight, we became increasingly interested in gleaning reliable, customer-driven data about their preferences. We knew doing so would provide valuable optics into what "customers" wanted versus what we've been delivering to the orthodontic "patients." Objectively measuring what patients really valued required us to find an alternative to the typical business survey system to fill that data void. When we did so, we were able to get a read on what fans of practices loved best and, conversely, what disgruntled patients disliked.

The Power of Online Reviews

You've probably heard business experts extol the value of online consumer reviews. Robert Cialdini's seminal work *Influence*, for example, teaches us the power of what he calls *social proof* and how it can be harnessed for business success. However, we had never seen anyone measure and quantify the different information written on reviews and what keywords might lead to a positive or negative orthodontic customer review.

Determined to find the answer, we picked a group of some of the most successful orthodontic practices in the country. We went through every one of those practices' Google reviews using a 0–5 scale and parsed out the best-rated (4s and 5s) and the worst-rated (1s and 2s) to identify any common themes. Next, we boiled down each review to one keyword contained in each review that summarized the overall tone of the review. What we found was that practices in the 4–5 range were rated highest for being friendly, professional, and kind.

Curious as to how Smile Direct Club® (SDC) customers compared to those reviewing orthodontic practices, we analyzed their consumer reviews and compared those to the reviews we'd parsed from the best orthodontic practices.

What we found astounded us! Some of the country's top orthodontic practice reviews and SDC reviews were nearly identical—with two very important exceptions: the words "quick" and "easy" did not appear at all on orthodontists' four-star and five-star reviews, but came in at number two and three on SDC reviews. The traits most orthodontists strive to offer—being friendly, professional, helpful, and comfortable—were ranked with relatively equal weight in both doctors' and SDC reviews. However, SDC was ranked extraordinarily high in convenience, while conventional practices were not. So all things being equal (in the eyes of consumers), the best orthodontists had less to offer—despite their perception that the only reason DTC providers win customers is the dramatic difference in price. Yet cost did not appear in the top ten responses at all!

4-5 Reviews

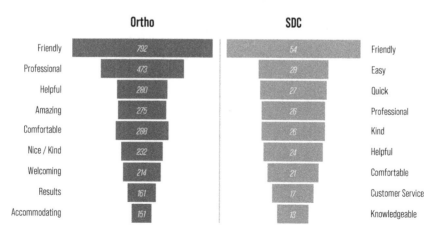

Ortho		SDC
Friendly	792	54	Friendly
Professional	473	29	Easy
Helpful	280	27	Quick
Amazing	275	26	Professional
Comfortable	268	26	Kind
Nice / Kind	232	24	Helpful
Welcoming	214	21	Comfortable
Results	161	17	Customer Service
Accommodating	151	13	Knowledgeable

The terms "easy" and "quick" offer some very interesting insight into what a large and growing population of prospective customers really want from orthodontic care. In other words, when competing with DTC businesses like Smile Direct Club, an orthodontist's clinical superiority doesn't actually give them much of an advantage—at least in terms of what drives people to write glowing Google or Facebook reviews. Since orthodontists know they offer clinical superiority, the majority of them have myopically responded to their DTC competition by assuming their superiority in that all-important category will win new patients. This being the case, they haven't seen the need to make any changes to the way they offer their superior clinical skills. In doing so, they've ignored the fact that convenience (easy + quick = convenience) is a premium to consumers and that those consumers don't have the knowledge base to differentiate excellent clinical skills from those provided at a DTC shop.

SDC Reviews

Friendly	54
Easy	28
Quick	27
Professional	26
Kind	26
Helpful	24
Comfortable	21
Customer Service	17
Knowledgeable	13

What they will notice right away is what they're missing from you—which is convenience. Why? Because typical orthodontic treatment is anything but easy and quick. When customers have to come to your practice twenty-five times to get treatment that is not easy and not quick, the takeaway is clear: it's essential to adopt a patient-centered approach that meets your patients where they want to be met (i.e., in a way that's convenient for them).

In other words, orthodontists must do better at making their customer's time a paramount consideration and push to improve their clinical efficiency while not sacrificing clinical results and to remember that customers want convenience in their new exams and to not have to wait. This consumer revelation is extremely important to your practice's growth. It should serve as a desperately needed wake-up call that alerts you to the changes prospective patients want you to make to accommodate their strong preference for easy and quick treatment—or risk losing their business. It tells orthodontists

IT'S ESSENTIAL TO ADOPT A PATIENT-CENTERED APPROACH THAT MEETS YOUR PATIENTS WHERE THEY WANT TO BE MET.

what they collectively need to identify (things that inhibit their clinical efficiency) and what solutions will make it easier for patients to do business with their practices. What's so enlightening about this information is that it allows a doctor to perceive their practice as patients do and not through the rose-tinted filter of their own confirmation bias. If you were to assess your own practice, for example, you might look at the attribute list we surveyed and say, "Oh yeah, we're all these things!" But would your patients actually agree with you? To find out, your first step is to verify that your practice as a whole is really offering the attributes prioritized by your patients. Although knowing what those attributes are is extremely important, you might need a decoder ring to understand how to implement them in your practice, so we'll explain how to do that.

What Patients Really Want

Don't let your confirmation bias lead you astray. It's not the leather upholstery or the new coffee bar you just had installed in your waiting room your prospective patients will truly value. Instead, let's take a quick look at each attribute we mentioned previously to make sure you understand what patients really mean when they say they prefer a practice that's friendly, easy, quick, professional, and kind:

Friendly

Being "friendly" with patients doesn't refer to talking about yourself as a form of self-revelation that invites them to open up in the same way. That's fine for neighbors or happy hour, but time spent in the exam room has a purpose for both the patient and the doctor: to determine whether treatment is necessary, how much it will cost, what steps are needed, and to identify any objections or obstacles the patient/customer may have to beginning treatment in your office. Like yourself, patients don't want to be there a Mom:ent longer than necessary, so information gathering should be friendly (read: people in the office should be kind and smile) but kept focused on the concerns and objections that brought the patient to your practice. Any small talk should be focused on finding out what they, not you, like to speak about.

Doctors, this also means you need to keep your explanations brief during exams. Don't spend forty-five minutes in the consult room talking dental jargon the patient doesn't understand just to show you know your stuff. Ninety percent of the time, your treatment coordinator can establish your skill and knowledge in a way that doesn't require you to utter one word about the mesiobuccal cusp or the physiology behind using nickel-titanium wires. Plus, the TC can usually explain processes in a way that's easier for a layperson to understand. In this effective scenario, the doctor's role is to do the diagnosis and treatment planning, treat the patients, and assist the remainder of the team when they're needed—not to do everything themselves—and that includes the sales process.

Plus, doctors, guess what? Much of the stuff you like to explain to the patient just confuses them and creates indecision that leads to more "Let me go home and think about it" outcomes. Even though you're trying to be helpful, any unnecessary explanation typically slows a patient's decision-making process and has zero impact on facilitating patients' treatments. Remember: You will deliver the same amazing clinical treatment, whether you tell them they need braces or whether you explain in detail the physiology behind frontal and undermining resorption. So it's best to keep your treatment suggestions simple unless patients specifically ask for further detail.

Easy/Quick

Start using online forms a patient can fill out on their phone ahead of time so that everything is ready and waiting for them when they arrive at the office. This is much better than handing patients that notorious, outdated clipboard, which requires them to wait for their insurance verification and other formalities to be completed. To break this convenience attribute down further, we found the reviews showed patients valued the following services:

- Contact information and schedule online
- Chat and text capable

- Exams available within seventy-two hours
- One-step consult
- Clinical efficiency

When considering same-day starts (which the team at Reynolds Orthodontics calls "same-day convenience"), a lot of doctors consider it a pushy sales tactic rather than a service that can make your treatment more convenient for busy consumers. Seen through this convenience lens, wouldn't you prefer to have as much as possible done while you're at an office rather than having to come back multiple times? Which sounds quicker and easier? Consider looking at all your office procedures through this lens and determine how many of your "That's how we've always done it" procedures may need to be updated, reimagined, and streamlined if you truly aim to be more convenient.

Have a staff member trained to answer phones and greet patients at the front desk five days a week and during every lunch hour when most patients have time off work to call. Since this kind of accessibility also makes your practice easier and quicker to use, it shows how these preferred practice attributes all tend to overlap. Additionally, until online scheduling becomes more robust, the only way prospective new customers can reach you is through the phone. Therefore, it's imperative customers can conveniently access you at a time that's best for them. Closing the phones for lunch to save on payroll because you aren't seeing clinical patients concurrently is incredibly penny wise and pound foolish.

Professional

Conveying a professional image means every member of your team needs to be neat and well organized, and that goes for the entire office environment too. Ensure office technology is kept current and updated, and use it to make confirmation calls, run on time, and maintain a good reputation by saying what you'll do and doing what you say. Remember, direct-to-consumer (DTC) shops have zero doctors and zero people with credentialed dental training, yet our surveys showed patients ranked them almost as "professional" as doctors with offices full of professional dental employees. How orthodontists envision professionalism and how customers do is clearly different.

Now that you know what services your patients want, you can expect to see your practice grow as you make the necessary changes to start offering those services to patients. Giving customers what they value, above any other factor, is the reason Smile Direct Club (an orthodontist's biggest competitor) could soon be doing more orthodontic starts than all of our profession put together. Keep in mind that those working in the customer-facing part of a DTC orthodontic company won't be orthodontists or dentists. They'll be someone they hired off the street with no professional credentials whatsoever, which means their "patients" likely won't know or meet whomever is actually doing their work. As you can see, the customer's threshold for "professionalism" is much lower than we all would like to admit. So why are so many people choosing DTC shops? If you guessed the reason was because they scored 4s and 5s on surveys indicating they were friendly, easy, quick, professional, and kind—you'd be right. Keep in mind that 7.2 percent of the total reviews we evaluated were only one to two stars, compared with 0.6 percent of the total number of orthodontists we looked at. Even though that number's a lot higher, it still means over 90 percent were four-to-five-star reviews.

What about Affordable?

Notice we never mentioned "affordable" (as in overall cost of treatment) and "cheap" as attributes patients valued on the surveys we assessed—because the customers didn't include those words in their reviews. So can you still say with a straight face that the *only* reason online providers are successful is strictly because of their lower price? Not convinced? Well, let's look at the ugly reality confronting conventional orthodontists. Patients don't find our services "easy" or "quick," and that's a huge reason why online providers have grown their market share significantly. What do you think? Are your treatments convenient? Since the average patient endures twenty-one office visits over the course of twenty-seven months of treatment, the answer to that rhetorical question is absolutely not! If they were honest, your patients would probably tell you their orthodontic care is more of a pain in the rear end rather than anything resembling "convenient." On that note, we suggest every treatment coordinator (TC) schedule a new patient exam (NPE) at a local Smile Direct Club shop and see how their experience during that NPE differs from the far lengthier process in their own offices.

Understanding why the DTC shop strategy of offering easy/quick treatment has been so successful is crucial for orthodontists aiming to compete with these corporate interests. Unfortunately, the closest thing to business advice doctors usually get is from their accountants. And that typically only happens when doctors go to their accountants and say, "Hey, Accountant! I want to make more money. How do I do that?" At that point, the accountant will take out your practice's profit-and-loss statement and tell you that your profits will go up when your expenses go down. That's a no-brainer, right? Not really, because the biggest expense on the profit-and-loss sheet is also most essential to your growth—namely, your team. And the majority of accountants will suggest you try to lower this cost by reducing the size of your team or by limiting their hours.

Buying into this line of thinking is a mistake because you'll end up treating your team like a liability. And you manage liabilities by managing their costs. If you ask your accountant, "Should we answer the phones at lunch?" they'll be likely to reply, "No! It adds to payroll!" But that would be terrible advice because taking calls during that time contributes to your growth and profitability. Let's look at why that is.

Number of NPEs Created by Time of Day

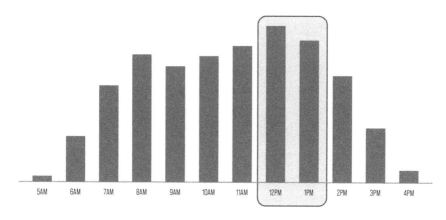

As you can see in the chart above, making the one simple change of answering your phones during the lunch hour can add 25 percent growth to your practice—which makes not answering your phones at lunch a very foolish decision. This is a great example of why you should start thinking of your team as your biggest asset and manage them accordingly by investing in them. Investing in your team will often mean hiring additional members and providing incentives and rewards—knowing you can expect a return on that investment. We'll be exploring how to add value for your team in the next chapter.

Takeaways for Adding Patient Value

- A patient-/customer-centered orthodontic practice is the biggest driver of performance.
- You need to know what your patients/customers want, then change your processes to add those things.
- Surveys show patients/customers want orthodontic providers to be friendly, easy, quick, professional, and kind—but, hey, that new coffee bar will make your team happier too.
- Collectively, orthodontists need to make it easier for their patients/customers to do business with them.
- If you haven't moved to a one-step consult, consider taking the necessary steps to offer that convenience. Your customers will be thrilled with the feature, and it will increase your conversions as well.

2

VALUE FOR YOUR TEAM

Hire good people and leave them alone.

—WILLIAM MCKNIGHT, PAST CEO OF 3M

The most important thing you need to remember from this chapter is that creating value for your team will add value to your practice. Period. It's the business law of cause and effect you probably never learned during your orthodontic training, but following it will unlock your practice's potential for growth and success.

Contrary to what you and your accountant may currently think, your team is not a financial liability—they are your biggest asset! And like any other asset, you need to invest in them if you expect a return on that investment. Adopting

> *CREATING VALUE FOR YOUR TEAM WILL ADD VALUE TO YOUR PRACTICE.*

and acting on that reality is going to be the crucial factor in determining how well you maintain and grow your business. We'll break that down for you and show you how to invest in your team by giving them what they need to feel motivated to work as a team in a way that will win you more patients and referrals. Doing so can turn your team into your best public relations talent available.

Once you start thinking about your team as the assets they truly are, you'll start seeing how incentivizing, rewarding, investing in, and multiplying your team pays you back. That's Business 101. In business development lingo, your team is referred to as "human capital," or an intangible asset, that won't show up on a company's balance sheet even though their contributions certainly will! Your team boosts your bottom line by fueling your practice's success with the combined economic clout of their experiences and skills: contributing their education, training, intelligence, physical and psychological health, loyalty, and dependability to your business.

Although a team's true worth to an orthodontic office may seem obvious, far too many doctors reverse this law of business success and treat team members like liabilities instead of the indispensable assets they are. This wrong-headed thinking originates in the very flawed perspective that the orthodontist is the center of the practice universe, and everything must revolve around his or her every thought, word, and need. But this view will block the growth and continued success of your practice in two serious ways:

First, being customer-centered is the secret to promoting growth in your business. We know you don't want to hear it, but it's really not about you, and your ego may be hurting your potential for success. You may be tempted to think of your office as your private kingdom, and your staff and patients are lucky to have you. Right? Maybe. But that mindset isn't the way to grow a business today! Your practice must focus squarely on what you can offer your customers and how well you can serve them. Doing that with excellence will inevitably drive and sustain your continued success as an industry. As we mentioned in the first chapter, the young adults and parents who are now your primary customers are a younger, tech-savvy demographic. You'll have to give them what they want, the way they want it—or risk losing out to the orthodontic providers who will, even though those providers may be offering a significantly inferior clinical outcome.

Second, it's the excellence of your team that's going to drive your continued success. The realization that your practice's prosperity is the direct result of your staff's efforts and not your own sterling, hard-won credentials may prove a hard pill to swallow. But it's true. Unlike a general dentist who does all the clinical work themselves, orthodontics is heavily delegated. Orthodontists only do a very small portion of the actual clinical work their patients receive, which means they rely on their team for virtually everything else that contributes to their business and clinical success. To be perfectly honest, you wouldn't accomplish anything without your team, right? So it makes perfect sense that your practice will benefit when you create value for your team in a way that improves their job performance—while driving your own success in the process.

Since your team is such a vital component of your business success, you'll obviously need to be intentional about how you seek out and hire talented people.

Strategic coach Dan Sullivan recommends a quick hiring hack that categorizes potential employees interviewing for a position into two groups: those with "batteries included" and "batteries not included." Think about that for a second. If you're interviewing someone, and you feel they would belong in a "batteries not included" bucket rather than a "batteries included" bucket, it's probably a good idea to look for someone else—especially for a clinical and TC position. Low-energy people will require you, or a member of your team (or both), to provide a lot of energy to bring them up to speed before they begin benefiting your team. Consider making "batteries included"—people who seem bright and energetic as a first impression—part of your hiring prerequisites.

Batteries aside, we think you'll agree it's hard to find the kind of skilled employees you're looking for. However, many offices wait until they really need a new team member before attempting to locate and hire one. If you need someone fast, the person who can walk and chew gum at the same time seals the deal these days. In other words, good support team personnel can be hard to find, especially since the "great resignation" we have all struggled through. But the acquisition, development, and retention of team talent is so critically important to an orthodontic practice's success; you don't want to lose those A players once you find them. So knowing what they want from you is crucial.

What Your Team Wants

When you think about creating value for your team, you probably assume a pay raise is the biggest motivator and what they want most. But you'd be wrong. Money is a "threshold motivator" that gets your team in the door every morning, but it won't get them motivated to really engage in their work roles and perform better on a consistent basis. That doesn't mean we're suggesting you don't have to pay your people well. On the contrary, it's imperative that your team is paid enough to be able to take care of their families without worrying about how they're going to pay their rent and buy groceries. And if you haven't adjusted your rate significantly from the impacts of inflation and the increased scarcity of employees, you need to. Yesterday. But similar to clinical outcomes, once you meet the baseline amount needed, dollars and cents don't have much effect on motivation. In other words, you can't solve your problems by throwing money at them. If you've been in business long enough, you've probably tried that already and can attest to the fact that attempting to solve problems with money alone only provides short-term relief—not long-term success.

Instead of money, it turns out that allowing people to be creative, productive, and self-directed is the reward that motivates them to perform their best. According to Daniel Pink, author of the book *Drive: The Surprising Truth about What Motivates Us*, "The secret to high performance and satisfaction—at work, at school, and at home—is the deeply human need to direct our own lives, to learn and create new things, and to

> ALLOWING PEOPLE TO BE CREATIVE, PRODUCTIVE, AND SELF-DIRECTED IS THE REWARD THAT MOTIVATES THEM.

do better by ourselves and our world." Distilling the previous statement into component parts, Pink asserts that what he calls autonomy, mastery, and purpose are the three elements that drive motivation most effectively. So let's examine those valued elements more closely to find out how you can give them to your team.

They Want Autonomy

Autonomy can be defined as a person's intrinsic desire to direct their own life. It may come as a shock, but your team wants autonomy just as much as you do. Why wouldn't they? As explained by Daniel Pink, your orthodontic team wants to be self-directed in the following ways: (1) what they do, (2) when they do it, (3) how they do it, and (4) whom they do it with. It isn't necessary for staff members to have autonomy in all four ways simultaneously all the time, but they should enjoy at least one in any given area of responsibility—and more, whenever it's feasible.

Of course, the opposite of your employees having autonomy is being micromanaged by their boss, even when you have no clue how to do what they're doing. If the doctor or the team leader(s) happen to have a personality that trends toward obsessive-compulsive, you might find it difficult to delegate anything. Your technical skills might be top-notch, but leaders who can't delegate successfully can get lost in the weeds trying to oversee the minutiae of their offices' day-to-day operations. Do you repair your own car or boat? The majority of doctors don't because they're way too busy providing the specialized skills they spent so many years acquiring and perfecting. But micromanaging doctors simply don't know what they don't know when they stray out of their area of training. Delegating key aspects of your business is a strategy you should be using already by letting your team do what they know how to do best, in a safe environment—without being subjected to constant scrutiny and distrust (a growth killer).

Let's face it, doctors: your team knows how to do a bunch of office practices and procedures you don't. You may have trouble turning on your x-ray machine or finding the wires you're looking for because you haven't a clue which drawer they're in. You probably remember that special visit on the weekend when no one from your team was there, and you got lost in your own office. After that, you should have understood that micromanaging the small details of a team member's job doesn't give them the credit they deserve for all the things they do that make your life easier and better. Hopefully, you realized that creating extra steps or unnecessary oversight does far more harm than just slowing them down—that it robs them of the motivation that drives the success of your practice and your profits.

We know you, as the doctor, are supposed to be the smart one, but your team members probably spend a lot of time thinking you're not the genius you think you are, thanks to some of the less-than-intelligent stuff you do. This is more than just an annoyance to your teams. By denying them autonomy, you're stripping away their inner motivation to do their jobs well. And many of them are talented in ways you aren't. Think about it. If you've ever had anyone micromanage you as you completed a task, you probably remember thinking, *If you're so smart, why don't you do it yourself?* We think you get the idea. None of you want that.

In *Drive*, Daniel Pink breaks down the independence everyone wants into what he calls the "4 Ts of Autonomy"—task, time, technique, and team. Let's apply these to your practice and take a look at each aspect so you can find ways to give your team members more choice in how they do their jobs.

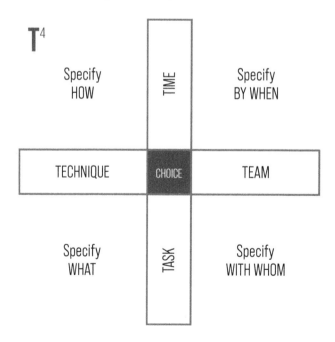

The 4 Ts of Autonomy

Task: Any activity an employee performs as part of their assigned role. To increase autonomy, you can allow more choice in the primary work they're doing or give them leeway to engage in practice-related work they're more passionate about. You might have a talented employee who just needs a little cross-training to excel in a role they would love to fill. Finding their work fulfilling matters more than salary to most people.

Time: How long it takes to complete a task. Deploying a results-only work environment (ROWE) provides more freedom for your team because it emphasizes that what gets done is more important than how long it takes. People aren't machines with "off" and "on" switches, and their productivity will ebb and flow. Being given a time goal allows them to work at their own pace to meet it.

Technique: The manner in which a job is done. Anyone who has a computer knows there are many ways to complete the same technical task. Everyone has their preferred method for working most efficiently, and your team's the same way. After you've told them what you want to be done, you should get out of the way and let them be creative and improvise within specified parameters. As long as you know team members have the needed skills to complete a task, letting them choose how to go about doing it allows the satisfaction of personalizing their job.

Team: The ability to choose who you work closely with. We all know people who rub us the wrong way, and working closely with them won't bring out the best in either one of us. Allowing your employees to choose who they team with simply acknowledges the reality that personal chemistry is a very significant factor in creating a productive work environment for everyone in your office. For example, in my own orthodontic office, I (Jamie) haven't been in charge of hiring for years since the team works more closely with new team members than I do. Allowing them autonomy with the task of hiring and training new team members leads to much more account-ability with the hiring process and a much happier team.

As you implement these four areas of autonomy in your practice, it's important to keep a couple of important qualifiers in mind. First, advise team members as to why a task is necessary, and explain its importance to the larger purpose and mission being achieved. Second, show empathy and admit when a task is boring, then offer incentives that can help offset the slowing effect of particularly tedious tasks by providing extra motivation. Third, teach your team a few ways to complete their tasks, then allow them to choose the method they prefer or to suggest a new one they think will work better!

They Want Mastery

Mastery in this context can be defined as the urge your team members feel to get better and better at something that really matters. But to assist them, you'll need to intentionally and consistently empower them to use their brains and think about the best way to master their orthodontic office tasks in new and better ways. Leaders in the office aren't the only ones who want to use their brains and col-laborate to improve the practice, although doctors are often the only ones who attend continuing education or developmental seminars. Your team

YOUR TEAM WANTS TO BECOME BETTER AT WHAT THEY DO, TOO, AND THEY'LL TRULY VALUE BEING GIVEN THE MENTAL AUTONOMY AND OPPORTUNITY TO ACHIEVE MASTERY.

wants to become better at what they do, too, and they'll truly value being given the mental autonomy and opportunity to achieve mastery they can use to creatively improve key aspects of their business.

49

Empower team members to use their brains and think—instead of being an automaton that mindlessly follows a formula or procedure.

In building Reynolds Orthodontics, we use a review concept called 360 reviews, which allows each team member to provide an anonymous review for the team member whose review it is. But unlike most offices, we have the team members review the doctors as well. And our experience with the team's responses validates the information found in Pink's book *Drive*. For example, here are some responses to the following question: "Does your doctor actively promote creativity and challenge you to perform at a higher level?"

Response 1: "For some of the responsibilities I have taken on, he actually asked me to come up with a good way to portray the information he wanted to analyze. He told me exactly what he was looking for and trusted in me that I would be able to come up with an effective and easy way to understand the needed analysis. He allowed me to use my creativity and skills to be a better employee."

Response 2: "[The doctor] asks many questions and makes me think it through and challenges me. I like learning that way. [It] makes me feel that he is invested in his team succeeding and learning as much as possible."

I moonlighted for a doctor in residency that would actually say, right in front of his team, "They're all a bunch of monkeys." I remember thinking: (1) Who hired them? and (2) Treat your team that way, and sooner or later, that's what you will get.

This is a vivid example of the absolute worst way an orthodontist can foster a growth mindset because it destroys the team mentality (not that you would, right?). It is probably the biggest motivation killer of them all, and it will hinder the profitability and success of any business. Food for thought: Do you call them your "staff" or your "team"? The answer may reveal the way your team perceives your level of respect for them.

Teaching people how to think without telling them what to think is your number-one job as the leader in your business. And it's the number-one critical element that ensures high performance is maintained when you're not physically there. One great way to do that is to invest in your team by bringing them to seminars and continuing education events. This shows you value your team at the same time it satisfies your team's desire to learn new things they can use to excel in their respective roles (thereby gaining mastery). Everyone loves to learn, and we all crave it, especially when that learning contributes to a tangible sense of success in our daily tasks. Building this kind of value for your team will pay off in spades.

Investing in your team by providing phone training, for example, is actually investing in your own success. If you were to record and score each new patient call, you'd find tracking the quality of your phone team is a difficult thing to measure. But tracking kept exam percentage (kept exams/scheduled exams) instead is an easy, albeit indirect, performance indicator that gives insight into the customer service your team is providing during new patient calls. Keeping your kept exam percentage above 90 percent is a good goal for verifying high-quality patient interactions with your phone team—both the phone team that fields the initial call and the consistency with which the preexam confirmation call is done (more on this later). If patients call in and get a very warm feeling about your office, they'll be more likely to keep their exam. But if they were turned off by your phone team, it's more likely they'll end up as no-shows, even though they booked exams. So avoiding that is a big deal, and phone training will help.

We get asked with some regularity who we recommend for phone training consulting. To date, Brian Wright (and his consulting company

New Patient Group) has the most comprehensive, thoughtful, and well-researched phone training we have come across, and we have recommended him with great success to many friends and colleagues. (That being said, I have no relationship with this company other than gratitude for the help it provided.) Basically, their training teaches you the psychology and mechanics behind predictably great new and existing patient calls and that a major key to raising your kept exam rate is to ensure the team members taking these calls have great energy and keep their calls short and sweet while providing a positive preview of what a patient can expect at their next visit. This proactively prepares them to start treatment. I would recommend their phone training system for people looking to improve their phone performance.

Offering this kind of intentional training is just one way to benefit your team (and your bottom line). Rethinking some of your current business habits that are restricting their success is another. Scheduling a longer appointment time than necessary, for example, or scheduling too many appointments before patients get their braces put on are two such hindrances. These inefficiencies make your team work harder and longer for what's a lot less convenient for your patients. Another example is allowing your wait list to exceed three weeks and booking prime-time appointment slots as though every one of them will show up. That doesn't work so well, either, requiring your team to make more follow-up calls that don't actually facilitate appointments. So what's holding you back? It's this: you probably prefer to stick with the way you've always done things because, honestly, going with the flow and the status quo is easier than trying to get better at something. Change is hard. What's more, just recognizing the need for change is hard. If it weren't, everyone would be equally successful. The obvious fact that's not true suggests the reason some practices are failing to grow during a time of increasing industry disruption is due to continuing the way they have always done things. Even if that's the case with your practice now, the ability to step back and admit the need for change is the biggest, most common hurdle to overcome to ensure your practice will grow and thrive in the future. Your ceiling for optimal performance will be higher once you've taken steps to switch away from your existing practices and start using more measurable, current, and team-oriented processes.

This is what is called a growth mindset. It's the belief your aptitude isn't fixed and that you can be better tomorrow than you are today if you're willing to put in the work, as described in Carol Dweck's must-read book *Mindset*. That doesn't necessarily mean working harder, but smarter. It also means adopting the mindset that no matter how well you may be doing currently, you can exceed that level.

The pursuit of mastery is an asymptote: something that never arrives at a final, fixed end point of a goal when it comes to growth. It's a term co-opted from analytic geometry—referring to a line that continually approaches a given curve but never meets it at any finite distance. Likewise, in a business context, an asymptote knows they can't, and won't, ever get all the way there in terms of achieving their full potential. Yet they keep striving for mastery anyway, knowing they can get incrementally better at whatever they're doing. Tiger Woods is a perfect example of an asymptote because he reconfigured his golf swing three times while he was already the number-one player in the world. In doing so, he perfectly exemplified a continual pursuit of mastery and the absence of any confirmation bias telling him he was good enough. Thinking, "I'm the best" would have kept him from getting any better.

You can start benefiting from these business principles by coaching the talented people you've brought on board in a way that fuels their continual drive toward mastery of their skill sets. Your team wants greater mastery of their respective skill sets because it enhances their personal proficiency and ability to succeed in the world of work. As each team member charts an upward trajectory toward greater individual success, they're contributing to the success and growth of the entire practice. It's a domino effect that starts when you add value to your team by adopting and applying these three business principles about mastery we've been discussing:

- Mastery requires a growth mindset.
- Mastery requires change and is *not* easy.
- Mastery requires being or becoming an asymptote.

They Want Purpose

Like everyone on the planet, your team members desire to find fulfillment in the service of something larger than themselves. And helping patients transform their lives by fixing their bites and smiles with orthodontics certainly fits that description. But what's amazing is that the helpful work your team does for patients can be transformative for each one of them too. They want to strive as individuals, getting progressively better in their respective roles while working together to accomplish a higher purpose for the patients they serve in a practice. People want to know that the mission of any business is more than making money.

YOUR TEAM MEMBERS DESIRE TO FIND FULFILLMENT IN THE SERVICE OF SOMETHING LARGER THAN THEMSELVES.

In an unsolicited post, Emily (one of my practices' TCs) expressed what team members everywhere want to experience with those they consider their work family:

> "I have never been so moved by a group of humans in my entire life," Emily wrote. "Every day I wake up, and I am

greeted with smiling faces, with true intentions, and with ideas for growth and upward change. I have never in my life been so shaken by my own thoughts of what my abilities were, my own bar that I never by any means set high enough. I am so grateful to work beside such strong mindsets, such empowering individuals with such a drive to do better and such a positive take on what's next. We work hard, and as I look in the mirror, because of the people I work beside, I know I can work harder [on] the areas in which I can improve and the takeaways for tomorrow. Thank you to each of you especially for challenging me in ways I did not know I needed to be challenged, for encouraging me through every learning curve, and for helping me to find a different mindset on the next go around. I could not be happier than I am with this family, and I am so looking forward to what we accomplish together in 2020."

The above post further validates the concepts we have discussed in this section. Could your team express the same kind of enthusiasm about working at your practice? If not, taking the actionable steps we've recommended in this chapter will add value for your staff in ways that will yield greater efficiency, effectiveness, and profitability to your business. And you won't have to wait for the next quarter to see those results. You can expect to see and feel them almost immediately.

Keep in mind that being smart is not the same as being success-ful, and that applies to you and every person on your team. Talent gives everyone in your office an initial advantage, but success results from each person using their talent and intelligence to identify what works (and what doesn't). Success also results from being willing to do the hard work of implementing needed changes to achieve better outcomes in every area of your business.

A big part of adding value to your team through a sense of purpose is establishing your authenticity as a leader who is truly committed to that higher perspective. If the team thinks all your leadership initiatives are just a cover to make you more money, fulfilling your team's deep-seated desire for purpose won't be credible or sustainable. Your job as a leader is to create real context for your team so they understand you're not asking them to excel at their jobs so you can afford a bigger house or fancier boat.

Dan Gilbert, CEO of Quicken Loans and owner of the Cleveland Cavaliers, said, "Money and numbers follow, they do not lead." More simply put, success does not result from simply trying to make more money because money is the consequence of providing value. That statement begs the question: What is true success? In this context, it's you and your team both committing to using the same method to achieve the same goal—pursuing an ever-higher level of excellence in how you serve your patients/customers. This altruistic, nonpredatory ethic rewards everyone involved, and it's a win-win-win for yourself, your team, and your patients. No one loses out or suffers loss at the expense of anyone else when a higher purpose is the overarching theme of your practice. Defining your practice's core values helps you do that and do it well.

Define Your Core Values

Once I learned more about management at my own orthodontic practice, I formed a leadership team and hired a business coach. The coach immediately directed this team to define our practice's mission and core values as our first task. Moving forward, all of our business decisions and behaviors have been assessed in light of those values.

CORE VALUES

DELIVER AMAZING
We strive for the 'WOW!' by consistently delivering above and beyond what is expected by our patients, team members, families, and community.

DELIVER WITH INTEGRITY
We are honest, forthcoming, and respectful, even when no one is looking.

Since my practice's primary core value is "Deliver Amazing," my team and I set about aligning every team member's efforts toward achieving that goal to benefit our patients. But getting everyone to work together cohesively as a team is something like going on a family road trip. Even though everyone's excited about where you're headed, getting there can be tricky.

In the business-management book *The Five Dysfunctions of a Team*, Patrick Lencioni advocates for reducing misunderstandings and confusion within a team by separately identifying and resolving the following five team dysfunctions: (1) absence of trust, (2) fear of conflict, (3) lack of commitment, (4) avoidance of accountability, and (5) inattention to results. Since all the other dysfunctions spring from the first one (an absence of trust), building trust among your team needs to become the priority. I found the only way to do it at my own practice was through mutual vulnerability and caring, and by making sure everyone felt heard even when we didn't agree.

In her book *Dare to Lead*, Brené Brown says, "I've yet to come across a company that has both a shaming, judgmental culture and wonderful customer service." And we've found she's absolutely right. It's a culture killer to take one team member's challenges and attribute them to everyone else. That's why course corrections discussed at your morning huddle need to be applicable to the whole team. Don't take the issues you have with one person and announce them at the huddle. Instead, make sure that happens during a direct and private conversation with the person who needs coaching. Each and every person wants to learn and achieve mastery in their roles, just as much as they want and need respect from their doctors, leaders, teammates, and patients. In fact, everyone learns and functions better in an atmosphere of mutual respect—the very thing that builds trust most effectively.

To give you an example, teaching one of your team members at the chair is one thing, but disrespecting their opinion in front of patients or other staff is another and causes the very loss of trust you need to establish. Be ready to adapt when you realize an unanticipated finding. Even the best doctor might miss something, and everyone makes mistakes. When they occur, truly great leaders take ownership of these mistakes, learn from them, and move forward without placing blame. Your team members are professionals like yourself. And they want and crave respect from doctors, teammates, and the patients they work on just as much as you do. Still not convinced?

Don't forget that one of the big reasons orthodontics is profitable is the doctor's ability to delegate many treatment responsibilities to various members of their teams. That arrangement works well as long as patients feel valued by the credibility of the care each and every one of your technicians is delivering. To learn how well I was doing at making my own practice team feel respected, I asked for their anonymous responses to this question: "Does the doctor show me respect? Does he keep critiques away from the chairside and use a respectful tone when explaining concerns and expectations?"

This was the typical answer: "If there is critiquing at the chair, you don't realize it's critiquing because it's so relaxed. Also, if it wasn't a huge deal, Dr. Reynolds just rolls with the punches. He doesn't stop me dead in my tracks and say, 'Take that wire out; you didn't do blah, blah,' so the patient continues to value me as their technician."

Everybody has their bad days, but leading your team well means setting the tone for the whole practice in a way that keeps everybody moving forward toward excellence. Once you've added value for your team in the ways we've discussed, they need to know they have a stake in the growth of your business. We'll show you how to communicate that with actionable steps which will not only add value to your enterprise and benefit your bottom line, but directly advantage your team by providing more opportunity for raises, job security, trips to conferences, team events, office remodels, and better technology. In the next chapter, "Value for the Enterprise," we'll discuss how to harness the power of adopting a growth mindset for your practice by using marketing and team incentives that will drive your success.

Takeaways for Adding Team Value

- Creating value for your team is investing in your own success.
- Provide your team career satisfaction by intentionally cultivating autonomy, mastery, and a sense of purpose.
- It's not about you (or your team). Putting the customer first is the secret to promoting growth for your business. It changes the dynamic of your work to one of service for others.

3

VALUE FOR THE ENTERPRISE

Often times we judge others on outcomes and ourselves on intent.

—DR. FADI BARADIHI

Now we're going to show you how to add value to your practice in a way that will stimulate growth for your entire enterprise. We know that's a topic of interest because we've heard so many doctors in orthodontics asking, "What's my practice really worth?" If that's a subject near and dear to your heart, you'll want to have a team that feels the same way. The problem is that a lot of practices have a team that doesn't share the fervor for the business's growth because they haven't been incentivized to do so. If they see fingerprints on the entrance's glass doors, for example, team members typically think, *Why should I care? You don't pay me enough to do windows. Why should it matter to me if the enterprise value grows? How is that meaningful to me?* They know the smudged glass will cause patients to wonder, "If the windows aren't clean, what else isn't clean?" But unmotivated team members won't care.

If you can tell your team lacks motivation and enthusiasm on the job, you've got a problem you need to address right away. We've already made the case for your team's central role in driving your success, so let's discuss how to get their goals to line up with those you have for your enterprise—because what's good for your business is good for them, too, and vice versa.

If your team seems listless, you may be one of those orthodontic doctors who "manage" their business by randomly treating whoever walks in the door and then sending a few muffins to the dentists around town to drum up more patients. That seriously flawed management style forces a doctor to hypermanage their bottom line to maximize profits. And you know what happens next, right? They'll try to wring more profits from their business by constricting the single most important factor to the growth of their business—their team. It's the reverse of everything they should be doing to build value for their patients, their team, and the enterprise itself. And it's going to be incredibly harmful to their practice's longer-term profitability. As we've already pointed out, the real wins to your bottom line come from increasing your top-line growth. Profits from patients who start at scale come in at a higher margin than the first patients you start. That margin is calculated by finding the difference between the sale price of a product and the variable costs associated with its production and promotion. Once your fixed expenses are paid (e.g., rent, team, utilities, and such) additional starts only cost you what you spend to start the patient: incidentals like wires, braces, glue, swag, eTC. So these additional starts are much more profitable to your bottom line.

Play Offense

In football, you've probably heard coaches say, "Defense wins cham pionships," and many times that's true. But even though you have a team, this winning strategy for football doesn't work in the orthodontic business. Going on the defensive and waiting around to see how the industry changes before responding to market trends is going to be a botched play in the new industry reality. What worked in the good old days may still seem

SWITCH TO A GROWTH MINDSET.
MANAGE METRICS.
PROVIDE TEAM INCENTIVES.

profitable to you and your practice, but we're here to warn you that your confirmation bias is giving you a false sense of security in light of the industry disruption that's occurring now. If you're about to retire anyway, that's fine. Enjoy. You may even get that once-in-a-lifetime multiple on your practice profits. But if you're not about to hang up your wire bending pliers, you'll need to be proactive about adapting to thrive in the new orthodontic landscape. We're about to show you how to do that by making three key changes to your practice:

- Switch to a growth mindset.
- Manage metrics.
- Provide team incentives.

Even though we're only recommending you change three things about your practice to stimulate growth, those three things will take time to implement and initiate. And someone on your staff will have to manage them once they're in place. At this point, you're probably wondering where you'll find the time to make any of these changes, even ones that are so important to your business's growth.

Consider Outsourcing

Historically, the orthodontic profession has been a kind of cottage industry in which practice owners were able to set up shop and run their privately owned businesses profitably. So outsourcing in this industry may seem unfamiliar or unnecessary to you. As an orthodontist, I felt that way too at first. But my perspective changed after we started using the software OrthoFi developed to outsource some of the mundane tasks in my own office. I knew we were onto something big when I saw how incredibly beneficial it was for my practice. By freeing my team from tasks that typically took little skill and a lot of time or those that focused on past agreements (collections), I was able to focus on growing future business. And it worked!

During the initial phases of OrthoFi's development, the original intention was to create software that was more of a lending platform than the operations solution it is today. But once we saw how streamlining patient onboarding fueled conversions and how removing the in-house burden of insurance, patient billing, and collections fueled practice growth—we switched gears. Now Oliver; Koz; our CEO, Dave; others; and I are gradually converting the leaders of our industry to a new growth mindset: one that acknowledges outsourcing as a better business strategy than the conventional operational systems of the past. In my own practice, for example, I've been able to reallocate my team's time and incentivize them by creating and offering new positions that fuel growth:

- **Pending coordinator:** Focuses on pending patient follow-up opportunities to convert more starts.
- **Marketing coordinator:** Manages patient relationships, nurtures and builds local referral practice networks, and spear-

heads community involvement, including advertising, events, and sponsorships.

- **Digital marketing coordinator:** Focuses on using SEO, capturing new digital, in-office content for social media, then designing, monitoring, and managing campaigns for Facebook and Instagram.

We've pointed out previously that today's orthodontic practices are facing fresh challenges in reaching and winning millennial patients (your primary future market). At the same time, many doctors are feeling the "squeeze" from low-priced, generic-care competitors who've already accessed that market quite successfully. The result? High-quality, technology-driven practices offering patient-friendly benefits like clear aligners and faster finishes are "stretched" between making patient payments affordable and managing default risk. We get it. That's why I personally found it such a relief when our company's software evolved and unexpectedly solved those squeeze-and-stretch issues in my own practice. And I haven't been the only one. Solid data shows the average practice using it grows 14 percent with only 3 percent more exams while enjoying over 40 percent of their conversions coming in the form of same-day contracts. And even if you don't use or decide to use a solution like OrthoFi, the concepts are indelible and should be adopted in any practice.

Go for a Growth Mindset

Outsourcing frees up the extra time you need to adopt a growth mindset and "play offense," reallocating the hours you'll gain daily to ramp up your marketing, sales process, and customer service. Investing time and energy in those specific areas is a great offensive strategy because that's what will drive your business forward. You don't want to get left behind using a passive "patients will fall in my lap" style that will leave you floundering in the new orthodontic landscape. To be honest, that kind of inertia is something every business has to fight. Failing to recognize market disruption and respond strategically has meant the demise of a lot of Fortune 50 companies, as well as countless smaller businesses. Knowing stagnation precedes business failure should galvanize you to assess your own mindset as an orthodontist.

The reality is that most of us resist change until it's forced upon us, but doing business reactively comes at a high cost. And the orthodontic industry, as a whole, is starting to recognize this truth—now that the number of new corporate players is growing so rapidly that conventional practices can't easily compete. The reason it's taken so long for orthodontists to acknowledge this trend is that the majority of practices are, or have been, successful. When you get up in the morning, drink your coffee, and head to work, you probably don't feel as though you're fighting for your business life because you've done so well financially.

The trouble with this rose-tinted view is that the majority of orthodontists don't know much about business development, sales, marketing, operations, or finance—and that's true for the entire gamut of practices, ranging from the smaller ones all the way up to the "mavens" of the industry. Since you're not going home hungry, you've probably assumed you're a natural when it comes to knowing how to run a business on the fly. Remember the confirmation bias we mentioned earlier? It's that rampant "We are profitable; therefore, we are indefinitely right" kind of thinking that persists because most doctors run a nice business, own a great house, and have a vacation place, or boat, to enjoy whenever they want. *We're obviously doing everything right,* they think. *We're living the good life. Right? Why can't we just continue doing what we've always done?*

Confirmation Bias Strikes Again

We hate to burst your bubble, but many of you are managing your businesses reactively instead of proactively—as if the primary market you're trying to reach is still the traditional baby boomers and Gen Xers who like to do transactions in person and watch cable TV instead of Netflix. And even though we know you're still seeing decent results in your pipeline, that flow is going to slow due to the massive industry changes happening right now. Patients no longer want to come in and spend a bunch of time having an orthodontic evaluation. And they certainly don't want to make several trips to your office before getting started. As the number of your more traditional patients diminishes, new generations are coming into the marketplace that don't want your service if they can do it online instead. They prefer snapping a few photos and having a quick online Zoom chat. That's because millennials and Gen Xers are fast information processors and multitaskers who are value oriented—preferring graphics over text, instant gratification, and frequent rewards. Just a heads-up: Boomers are adopting these preferences, too, and aren't far behind them. If you want validation, just think about how frequently you use voice mail versus text messages. Then, consider there is still a large portion of dental practices that use fax machines …

Your corporate competitors are already leveraging these generational traits to drive their success. Likewise, they're pricing their services to reflect the fact that Gen Xers and millennials don't have the accumulated wealth of the baby boomers preceding them. They know there will be fewer orthodontic treatment dollars to go around as boomers are replaced by their younger generational cohorts. Consider these numbers from the financial and technology services company Kasasa® to see for yourself:

- Baby boomers' average net worth is $1,066,000; median net worth is $224,000.
- Gen Xers' average net worth is around $288,700; median net worth is $59,800.
- Millennials' average net worth is about $76,200; median net worth is $11,100.
- Gen Zers' average net worth is still unknown with no net worth or career yet.

Notice the trend? To cope and grow your practice in the future, you'll need to have a solid business response and a planned strategy for efficiency and growth directed at your primary, decision-making orthodontic market. That market will be comprised of millennials born between 1980 and 1994, who are currently between twenty-six to forty years old, plus young adults in their early twenties from the Gen Z group, born after 1995. Both groups "live" online, and the younger they are, the more they want to do everything faster. If you make them wait ten seconds, that's too long. These digital natives have grown up breathing instant online connectivity the way previous generations used newspapers, magazines, and landlines. The postal service is now known as "snail mail," and it's fighting a losing battle trying to compete with the instantaneous convenience and affordability of emails and texts. Even speaking by phone is increasingly avoided by millennials.

As our industry evolves and our DTC competitors are marketing themselves as convenient, fast, and affordable, many orthodontists are still functioning like the snail mail no one wants to use anymore.

Instead of feeling insulted, consider the fact that a lot of practices only stay open four days a week, Monday through Thursday. And on those four days, a lot of offices don't answer their phones during lunch hour—the very time it's most convenient for their patients/customers to call them from work. Trying to call when they get off work doesn't work, either, because the majority of privately owned orthodontic offices close for the day at 4:30 or 5:00 p.m., only a few hours after schools let out.

A doctor's office is just about the only local business you call at lunch and get a voice mail message instead of a live person. But your competitors will be available twenty-four seven and win your main market for patients—younger millennials—by doing things in the new-school way they prefer. Do you see the problem? If you want to live your new growth mindset, your practice will have to change to be readily available for inbound interest in a way that's accessible, easy, and quick. You don't want to lose all those new starts, right?

You may not like where this is going, and you're probably already trying to think about ways you can attract the business of ninety-five million millennials by improving areas you're already good at, or enjoy doing, such as adding a bigger-screen TV or leather-upholstered furniture to your waiting room. But that's still contending with the marketing problem you face in what's basically the same, self-glorifying way you've tried to appeal to patients in the past, thinking, *I'll make my office look nicer or more welcoming.* You're simply thinking about the wrong things and what makes you look better and more impressive. Instead, think about what the patient wants and design the whole experience around them—not around your four-day (or less) work week and your reluctance to extend your office hours or cover the phones at lunch, in the evenings, and on weekends.

If Twitter data from 4.8 million users is any guide, peak posting globally occurs between noon and 1:00 p.m. each day. In addition to jumping on social media, it's only logical that's the time your prospective patients are most likely to be looking for a doctor. Yet that peak hour is the exact time no one's answering your phones. Do you see where we're going with this? It's just one example of how contending with industry disruption in a competitive way means you'll have to adapt and change—or be prepared to suffer loss. Ignoring the problem completely and planning your three-day weekend means you're definitely suffering from a bad case of confirmation bias.

Of course, it's impossible to know how well your orthodontic business is actually doing without a way to measure that. Business legend Peter Drucker famously stated, "You can't manage what you don't measure." Before we piloted the beta software for OrthoFi at my own practice in Detroit and Jeff Kozlowski's practice in Connecticut, for example, my team thought our TC performance was top-notch since we were the biggest office around (a clear case of economic confirmation bias). But the software showed us we were only operating at a 37 percent forty-five-day treatment-recommended conversion (TRC) rate. My first reaction was to call our company's CEO, Dave Ternan, thinking the algorithm providing the assessment was faulty. But it turned out our low TRC numbers were accurate, and that our own poor assessments had lulled us into a false sense of security. On the bright side, knowing what's going wrong is the first step to making it right. And the sooner the better!

> *KNOWING WHAT'S GOING WRONG IS THE FIRST STEP TO MAKING IT RIGHT. AND THE SOONER THE BETTER!*

DID YOU KNOW?

Practices that actively use the software's pending management tool see 18 percent higher conversion rates? On average, that's over $160,000 of annual production! The tool facilitates that higher conversion rate by using easy-to-track reminders with full visibility throughout the office so no patient falls through the cracks.

OK, numbers are great for measuring things like performance and productivity. But the team members responsible for generating those numbers are individuals with their own emotional and intellectual needs. To ramp up and stay competitive, your team requires incentives that are personally meaningful to them. They must know (beyond the shadow of a doubt) that your business's growth will offer them more opportunities for raises, job security, technology, trips to headquarters, team events, and an office remodel providing a great work environment. You've heard the saying "Hitch your wagon to a star," right? That's how your team needs to feel about your practice. As your business grows, its strength and stability should benefit your team in equal measure. In other words, the success of the enterprise means success for them too. Once that's understood, a doc and their team will be sharing the same goal—continued success and growth for your/their shared enterprise. To bring that about requires marketing.

Show How You Help Patients

Does the idea of marketing yourself or your practice seem unprofessional? If so, you've probably seen a tangible decrease in new patients over the last few years. But if the opposite is true, and you really like marketing all the good things your orthodontic practice offers—we're certain you're seeing it grow. Like it or not, however, you'll have to get really good at marketing and sales if you hope to compete and take your practice to the next level. Having worked so hard to get where you are, marketing gives you the chance to show what you can do and what you have to offer to a patient/customer who needs your services to get a beautiful, healthy smile. When a patient says "yes" to treatment, it simply means you get to use your expertise to give them what they already want. And remember, Doctor: you have unimpeachable integrity and only recommend treatment to cases in which you would recommend the same to your family. *You and you alone are in charge of what you sell.* And if you are practicing as you should, they should buy what you are selling because it is both good for them and the best place around to get the treatment. This patient-centric focus is the ethical connection between marketing, sales, and the growth of your business. In other words, marketing communicates how you can help them reach their goals.

Marketing Is Your Message

Your marketing is the message you put out about your business to explain why what you provide is important to your customers. Simple, right? A customer wants to know, "What are you about, why should I care, and why should I spend my hard-earned dollars with your company?" Your marketing should be intentionally designed to explain that you can give them what they want better than anyone else. If you can't answer the question, "Why should my prospective customer choose me over others?" you need to figure that out ASAP. Here's a clue: you'll first need to know what your customer/patient wants, then focus on telling them how you're going to provide it. That will mean making decisions about how to connect with them to let them know what you're offering. Remember when we said freeing up time for marketing positions in your practice was a good thing? Change the word "good" to *necessary*.

Sales Is Offering to Serve

If you do a good job creating a valuable marketing message, you will have prospective customers calling your office to investigate becoming a patient. We define "sales" as the process of shepherding those prospective customers into becoming actual customers. That's it. There need not be anything slippery or deceptive here, because you're never going to offer anything to anyone that they don't need or that doesn't benefit them. Rather, you're going to be using your expertise to give them what they want and need in the best way possible. Logically speaking, you know there are a lot of people in your community who want to get braces for themselves or for their children over the next year—whether they've had an exam or not. So if your marketing puts you in front of them in an interesting way before your competition does, they're going to come to you first. But here's the problem. You're not really competing against other local orthodontists, or dentists trying to hit their production goals, or even against DTC industry disruptors. Honestly, what you're really competing against is ad space and the myriad advertisers who are vying for your patients' discretionary spending ranging from home

> *WHAT YOU'RE REALLY COMPETING AGAINST IS AD SPACE AND THE MYRIAD ADVERTISERS WHO ARE VYING FOR YOUR PATIENTS' DISCRETIONARY SPENDING.*

improvements to snowmobiles, to Nike Jordans, to Apple computers, Botox, Disney, or anything else on Amazon.

Have we made our point? It's an advertising war zone out there! You have so many marketing options to choose from, describing them all is beyond the scope of this book. But at Reynolds Orthodontics, we are utilizing the following eight marketing strategies as of this writing:

1. Internal Marketing

This is the best type of marketing because it conveys authenticity. Treat your patients extraordinarily well, and don't be afraid to ask them to refer their friends. Have contests and host patient appreciation parties, concert giveaways, and just about any other event that's fun to spread goodwill (and name recognition) throughout your community.

2. Website

Hiring a professional website company to design and maintain your practice's website is necessary to keep it up to date and benefit from dependable web hosting, search engine optimization, mobile friendliness, appointment reminders, online scheduling, and VOIP services.

3. Logo and Brand

Investing in your practice's logo and branding is a visual way to consistently represent your orthodontic practice and convey its "personality" as warm, accessible, progressive, and leading edge.

4. CRM

Using a tech-enabled customer relationship management (CRM) solution (I use OrthoFi) will enable you to combine your CRM with a revenue cycle management (RCM) system. Doing so will help your practice start more patients by managing their insurance billing and collections most efficiently and allow you to focus more of your team's efforts on work that will grow your practice.

5. Facebook and Instagram Pages

Enlisting someone on your team to create authentic videos, photos, and captions showcasing your practice is better than using generic content. Producing and writing this social media marketing gold "in house" is best. If you make the mistake of outsourcing these channels, your practice will quickly seem inauthentic, so hire someone in your office, and put them in charge of making you look great. Also, remember to be yourself. Not everyone is cut out to be a social media darling. But every orthodontist can develop very enriching educational content to answer the most common orthodontic questions. Start with education before trying to be the next YouTube sensation or creating the next viral music video with dental lyrics. There is only one Grant Collins and only one Cole Johnson. We are all best served to remember that authenticity is by far and away the most persuasive strategy.

6. Referral Marketing

Although not the sure thing it was ten to twenty years ago, professional referral relationships still need to be nurtured and cultivated. Even doctors who do their own orthodontics will send you the hard cases. But try to be creative, and don't just send over a box of doughnuts with your business card stapled to it and expect the patient referrals to start pouring in.

7. Team Incentives

Replace discount promotions with team incentives. After adding up all your office's discounts, divide it by two, then put it into a kitty to reward each member for their performance. Or figure out your own way to reward performance and align the team goals with the practice goals. You'll be amazed at how much better everyone performs.

8. Paid Search

Like it or not, SEO is increasingly ineffective, and paid ads work, but are expensive. However, if done well, the ROI for paid search is impressive. If you're playing this game for keeps, be sure your phones are on point and your conversion is dialed in before you waste a bunch of money on ads—only to have your phone or TC skills waste the opportunities the ads provide. Also, outdated websites don't play well with paid search. So make sure your website is up to date before looking at this bucket.

Initiating these eight marketing essentials requires some investment, but is critical to growth. With the time you save outsourcing, you can reallocate those hours and focus your energies on these key marketing areas. As your team's leader, that's where you need to focus your energies to grow your enterprise, and it will benefit both your team and you.

Keeping Score with TRC

Since you're competing with other orthodontic providers, you'll obviously want to know what their marketing looks like so you can do it better. But to find out how well your own is working, you'll need to use timely and relevant data analytics to find out what's working for you and what's not. As the previous quote from Peter Drucker emphasized, you can't get better at something without keeping score. That's why your treatment-recommended conversion rate (TRC=#starts/#recommends) is so critically important. It will be the scoreboard that indicates how effectively you are communicating your marketing message—the message that tells your patients/customers why the services you provide should be important to them. In other words, TRC measures how likely someone is to say, "Yes!" when you recommend treatment; it acts as an objective measure of the effectiveness of your marketing message and sales process.

Across the one-thousand-plus practice locations using our software in the United States, the average TRC is 64 percent, with a low of 20 percent and a current high of over 90 percent. Of the many factors involved in increasing TRC, none is more important than the percentage of starts who sign the same day it's recommended (same-day contracts). Of course, an office's ability to schedule that patient to start the day of the recommend— and the quality of your practice's follow-up process for patients who need time to "think

> *YOUR TRC WILL BE THE SCORECARD THAT INDICATES HOW EFFECTIVELY YOU ARE COMMUNICATING YOUR MARKETING MESSAGE.*

about" your recommendation before starting treatment—will impact your TRC rate. OrthoFi software is designed to increase TRC because it's built to drive more same-day starts with its mobile-friendly intake forms and the way it calculates accurate insurance benefits and patient responsibility fees before the consult. Again, using OrthoFi isn't requisite of great sales performance, but utilizing the concepts OrthoFi was built around is.

An essential part of playing offense is setting expectations through the confirmation call process. For the greatest impact, these calls should be scripted and carefully planned like every other aspect of a successful practice with three main goals in mind: (1) to be a personalized reminder call to increase the likelihood they make the appointment or to reopen the appointment slot if they have decided to cancel without telling you; (2) to encourage the patient to fill out any unfilled forms—the key component of which is completing the insurance information so a benefits check can be done prior to their exam; and (3) to set expectations for the exam process and let them know that, should treatment be recommended, the office has set time aside to make starting treatment convenient. In order for same-day starts to be viewed as convenient and not pushy, it is imperative the prospective customer has time to consider starting that day before they arrive at the office. If they hear about same-day service for the first time in the consult room, it is nearly impossible for the TC not to come across as pushy. People and technology need to work together synergistically. You must encourage your same-day starts (SDS) by getting everyone in your practice onboard with a team approach that conveys customers/patients come first and that giving patients what they want conveniently is your highest priority. This better, more fulfilling mindset creates a shared goal between your patient/customer and your orthodontic team. All the data shows your patients want quick, easy, and convenient treatment, and that's the very thing you want to give them.

As we pointed out previously, once you know what your patients want, your job is to figure out how to give it to them in a competitive and ethically persuasive way. This perspective changes the sales dynamic into a service dynamic, which is more satisfying for everyone involved—you, your team, and most importantly, your patients. It converts the seemingly predatory dynamic of "selling something" to a potentially unwilling patient into the positive dynamic of providing a service that gives them what they want in the best way possible. Since you know your practice is better able to offer quality orthodontic care than competitors, you can take the high ground of offering service integrity others can't. Consider this: Do you feel it's more ethical to wait for patients to walk through your door, and thereby risk them being treated by providers doing lesser work? If you do, at least now you'll know why you're not performing as well as other practices who are playing offense by proactively managing expectations and objections.

In part II of the book, we'll explain the concept of intelligent flexibility and show why it's so important you understand it and put it to use ASAP. This is the concept that orthodontists need to be more flexible with payment plans to get patients to accept treatment. The problem is that forcing your entire customer base into plans that require 20 percent down, then compressing the rest of the payments into treatment time, is outdated. But simply lowering payments increases default risk. Next, we will outline the need to know about financial payment solutions that maximize conversion and minimize default risk while balancing and optimizing the three levers of flexibility, cash flow, and risk management.

Takeaways for Adding Enterprise Value

- Motivate your team to care about your practice as much as you do by adopting a growth mindset, managing metrics, and using team incentives.
- Grow your business by taking these three steps:

1. Launch a robust marketing effort.
2. Make great customer service your priority.
3. Ensure a high, consistent conversion percentage by proactively building value in the service you provide and by proactively managing the potential objections of your customers.

- Manage your metrics by using data analytics to convert staff time for marketing and to tell you what's working and what's not. Your TRC rate will measure the effectiveness of your marketing message and sales process.

Part II
INTELLIGENT FLEXIBILITY

I n this second part of the book, we sum up the benefits of the powerful business approach we've dubbed *intelligent flexibility*. We'll explain how using it can enable you to balance your practice's growth, cash flow, and risk while making your treatment more affordable for the patients who need it. It's an essential business strategy for orthodontists feeling squeezed between the higher expense of treatment using digital workflows and the lower cost and quality of such treatment being offered by DTC shops and others. Confronted with increasing industry competition, many orthodontists feel trapped between two difficult options: either risk losing patients by charging higher up-front costs and monthly payments for popular new treatments or face financial risk that hurts their practice. Such risk is the downside of winning patients by offering lower up-front treatment fees and the extended financing associated with poor cash flow and payment default.

What many don't realize is that intelligent flexibility provides a third option that's already resolved that business conundrum in hundreds of orthodontic practices. This third option is an effective, data-driven strategy that allows orthodontists to continue putting quality first by offering top-notch care, while also lowering their down payment for digital orthodontic treatment—and do it without risking patient default. If that sounds too good to be true, it's not. But to understand how and why this third option works, we need to clear up a few of your misconceptions.

One such misconception is that your orthodontic consumers (or any consumer for that matter) will choose a provider based on price alone, despite the mountain of data across all industries proving otherwise.

THAT DATA CONCLUSIVELY SHOWS COMPETING ON OVERALL PRICE ISN'T NECESSARY, BUT OFFERING PAYMENT TERMS CUSTOMERS CAN AFFORD UP FRONT AND MONTHLY IS CRUCIAL!

In case you haven't noticed, the days are gone when most of your prospective patients can afford to, or will choose to, pay 20 percent down and then compress the rest of their monthly payments into a plan that coincides with the length of their treatment—especially now that treatment times are getting shorter. But simply lowering down payments isn't the answer either because that tactic increases the risk of default. Intelligent flexibility is the solution to this dilemma since it minimizes and balances default risk with three powerful levers: flexibility, cash flow, and risk management. In the following chapters, we'll take a deep dive into why this approach works so well by showing you the numbers proving its efficacy, then explain how to implement it in your own practice.

4

PRICE VERSUS AFFORDABILITY

"Do not compromise on the quality and your
customers will not negotiate on the price."

—AMIT KALANTRI

Price is the five-letter word most of us don't want to talk about, but it
doesn't have to be that way. If you communicate your value proposi-
tion clearly and consistently, the price of your treatment is going to
be much less of an obstacle to your patients than you think—as long
as your fee is set using a few logical guidelines. For starters, it's a good
idea to know the "average" fee being charged by other doctors in your
practice area, but not so you can beat their price. We point that out
because we know that a lot of orthodontists fear pricing themselves
out of the market if their services are priced higher than their com-

petitors. But that fear isn't based on the facts: current data confirms the majority of people actually prefer higher-quality orthodontics to cheap orthodontics when seeking treatment—as long as it's affordable.

In fact, among over a hundred practices we evaluated, the one charging the lowest average fee had the lowest treatment-recommended conversion rate or TRC. We weren't surprised, since we already knew an excellent conversion rate is the product of much more than any one single factor—including cost. As long as you price your treatment within an average range (between $5,300 and $7,000 depending on your local area), there is actually very little correlation between price and conversion rate. That fact alone is very important to remember because the first thing orthodontists think they should do when they get nervous about their conversion rate is to lower their fees.

The moral of this pricing story is that you can't build your growth strategy on low fees and expect to win the day, and the numbers prove it. The reason is that consumers usually equate the price of something with its quality, whether they're buying a car, a home appliance—or healthcare. According to a study by Narayanan Janakiraman published in the *Journal of Marketing Research*, people expect to pay a higher price for higher quality and associate lower prices with lower quality. What wine people choose to buy is a great example of this tendency. People will pay extra for quality wine if they have confidence the quality is really there in the bottle. They could pay less for cheap wine, but they don't. This was proven during wine taste tests when tasters were told one bottle cost $100 and a second one only $15. Then they switched the bottles without telling the tasters. Amazingly, 80 percent of the taste testers always picked the wine they thought was more expensive, regardless of which wine they were actually tasting. In some ways, orthodontic treatment is similar to wine in that the average consumer can't evaluate true quality, so the only way they can ascribe quality is by price. Essentially, they presume that the higher fee means higher quality. So don't be afraid to set your fees at the higher end, as befits the superior treatment you provide. Our goal for the orthodontists we advise is to deliver outstanding value to each and every patient they see. For that, command the highest fees, but at the same time leverage the principles of flexibility to also be the most affordable.

Affordability

How can an orthodontist charge higher fees and still be the most affordable option? The mystery is solved when you grasp the concept that affordability is distinct from price. As an orthodontist from Detroit, I tend to relate marketing realities within the context of the auto industry. Carmakers

HOW CAN AN ORTHODONTIST CHARGE HIGHER FEES AND STILL BE THE MOST AFFORDABLE OPTION?

have grown over the last decade by understanding that regular people want to drive premium cars, but they'll only do that if the monthly payments are within their budget. That's why leasing is up nearly 50 percent from ten years ago, and why nearly half of all luxury car sales are leases. High-end car companies were having an increasingly difficult time selling big-ticket luxury cars with high monthly payments until they figured out a solution. When they created leases that had lower monthly payments, lots of additional people chose to drive those nicer cars. It turns out people are more concerned with quality and affordability than the overall cost of something over time. Growth in car leasing proves that consumers will pay a higher price for better quality if it's affordable monthly.

Before I knew that, I followed the conventional wisdom of the leading practice-management gurus and only offered two financing options to new patients: they could choose payment in full (with a courtesy discount) or opt to pay a 15 to 20 percent down payment with monthly payments divided up to coincide with the length of their treatment time. When the recession hit Detroit (and my practice) in 2007, I added the third option of a low, or zero, down payment option, and even farmed out a few lower-income patients to a third-party financing company (e.g., Care Credit) despite punitive interest rates. Even so, my team and I found negotiating the terms of payment with a patient was often the most uncomfortable part of the consultation process. For many orthodontists, it probably still is.

Although there are a variety of ways to present treatment fee options, a lot of the best-performing offices still engage in some active negotiation with patients over their down payments and monthly payments. The problem is that this still requires a very efficient infrastructure and a talented, sales-savvy treatment coordinator. So if your TC thrives on actively negotiating down payments and monthly fees, you're one of the fortunate few. But the majority of offices aren't so lucky and simply default to offering patients two or three payment options as I did. As a result, my practice was able to tread water but never made a breakthrough in growth until my team and I changed our philosophy, acting on data trends Oliver and I have since used to prove every orthodontic practice should expand their patients' financing options ASAP. We are working hard to dispel some of the down payment and monthly payment myths hurting the growth of orthodontists everywhere.

5

FLEXIBILITY EQUALS PROFITABILITY

In God we trust, all others bring data.

—WILLIAM E. DEMING

Most of you probably don't teach yoga or Pilates in your waiting rooms, so you may be wondering what flexibility has to do with how you offer your orthodontic expertise to patients. In this case, we're referring to financing flexibility (i.e., the willingness to change or compromise the way you charge your patients for treatment). Getting flexible in this financial operations area will not only drive your practice's growth but ensure more patients are actually able to afford the treatment they want and need from you. That's what the data shows, and those numbers are well worth examining because they prove there is a direct relationship between how flexible you make your patient financing and the number of new patient starts you'll see at your practice.

After big data sets revealed this cause-and-effect relationship between financing flexibility and practice growth, a lot of us wondered how we'd missed seeing the connection. Unfortunately, too many doctors still aren't aware of how well this business principle actually works when it's implemented properly. Thanks to the way flexible financing spurs practice growth, orthodontists who use it find they're able to offer high-quality treatment to many more people than they could otherwise—thereby fulfilling their objective of becoming orthodontists in the first place. Making the decision to offer flexible payment options is a crucial first step to accomplishing that lofty goal in a profitable way. But doing so doesn't mean defaulting to what we call rote flexibility, or offering low monthly payments and extended financing to everyone. In other words, flexible financing isn't starting treatment for anyone who walks through your door, willing to put $99 down and pay $99 a month. There's no choice or customization in that kind of approach. Instead, it's imperative you determine which patients really need more affordable financing, and to what degree, before they can begin treatment. Once you've assessed that for each patient, you can provide a customized structure for the amount of their down payment and monthly payment.

> *"AFFORDABLE" DOESN'T HAVE TO MEAN "CHEAP." IT MEANS ALLOWING PATIENTS TO MAKE OPEN-ENDED FINANCING CHOICES FROM A WIDE SPECTRUM OF OPTIONS IN A REVOLUTIONARY WAY.*

Keep in mind, however, that "affordable" doesn't have to mean "cheap." It means allowing patients to make open-ended financing choices from a wide spectrum of options in a revolutionary way—one requiring you to offer genuine flexibility "on demand," as opposed to rote flexibility "by default." In other words, financing works better for everybody when the decision-making process is balanced and individualized by determining which patients really need a lower down payment or monthly payment. But don't expect to reap the benefits of this kind of flexibility by simply changing all your patients' down payment options to range from $0 to $250 down and spreading their payments over thirty-six months. That's the rote flexibility we just warned you about, and although it may increase starts, it can create unpleasant cash-flow issues. Using different financing criteria for different patients allows you to avoid low cash flow while accommodating individual patients most responsively.

The Culture of Now

Increasing a practice's SDS rate is arguably the single most important key to growth because 100 percent of SDS patients convert from being potential patients to actual patients. In other words, patients who get their braces on and begin paying for treatment the same day of their new patient exam (NPE) are considered SDS patients. This is the best-case scenario for orthodontists who know practice growth is directly proportional to a higher SDS rate. It's not only the fastest way to grow your practice, but an SDS is also the most convenient for your patient.

When an SDS doesn't occur, many doctors simply aren't aware of the conversion power of their next best option—offering flexible, attractive financing terms that prompt patients to sign a contract the same day of the NPE. Why is this so important? Because 98.6 percent of the patients that sign a contract on the day of their consult will actually start treatment. If a patient just schedules a return appointment to start treatment later, the conversion rate drops to 80 percent—which is still pretty good. In fact, it's a much better rate than the average practice enjoys.

CONVERSION RATES

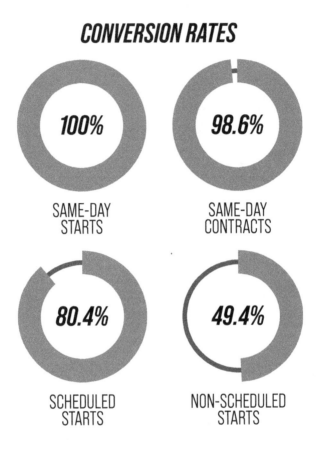

But when patients leave your office without any of these commitments, your conversion rate is likely to drop to under 50 percent. Although these four scenarios imply consumer behavior is driving the high or low rate of conversion, that's not the reality.

Provider availability to initiate a patient's SDS treatment is reflected in those statistics, too, meaning a patient can be ready for an SDS, but the doctor and their team aren't. A practice's operational capacity to accommodate SDS patients takes the implementation of intentional steps we'll be discussing later.

Booking Window

For now, it's imperative you understand that flexibility isn't just about money and payment but is about being flexible with your time as well. More specifically, it has to do with a concept we call *booking window*, which measures how quickly you can get a prospective patient in for an evaluation from the day they call requesting one. As the booking window increases, you effectively create a wait list for new patient exams, which may be good for your ego but is definitely not good for your growth goals. Shrinking long booking windows may require opening another TC column during high-demand times, becoming more efficient with exams so that you can offer more per day, or intentionally leaving some appointment spots open in the middle of the morning when people are most likely to want to see you. It may also mean employing a "floating" clinician who's available for on-demand SDS patients instead of being assigned to a specific column of work.

If you're not able to see a prospective patient for a new patient exam at the Mom:ent they call and set an appointment, their likelihood of becoming a patient decays by about 8 percent instantly. When patients call for an appointment, they're indicating they want to start their orthodontic process right away. So don't keep them waiting. To help with this, we've found the majority of practices can shorten their new patient exam slots and open up additional time for appointments if they avoid conversations touting their medical expertise and focus on what the new patients want instead. Nearly all high-performing offices are able to offer exams that take fewer than sixty minutes, with an increasing number moving toward using shorter forty-five-minute, or even thirty-minute, exam slots.

That's a smart move, and the graph below shows why: if the booking window extends and new patient exams don't happen within three weeks of patients' initial calls to schedule them, 3 percent of children's NPEs and 11 percent of adults' NPEs won't occur at all. After a month, those numbers increase to an 8 percent loss for children and 14 percent for adults not keeping their NPE.

KEPT EXAM DECAY

(Days Between Date Scheduled and NPE Date)

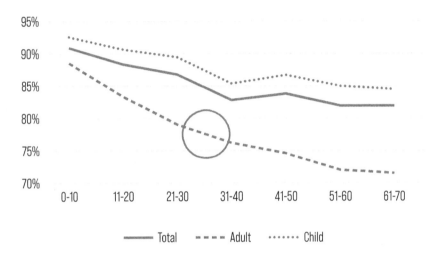

To delve even deeper, we recently analyzed data to help us understand the recent erosion of Kept NPE Rate, which has dropped almost 8 points (82 to 74 percent) since 2019. The primary factor we identified to explain this trend was an increase in booking window length. The key to unlocking the insight was to filter our population into two cohort groups: (1) all patients who did convert successfully and started treatment, and (2) those patients who either did not convert or who never showed up for their exam. This filter created a demonstrable separation between groups 1 and 2, well beyond standard deviation.

DAYS TO EXAM SCHEDULED VS KEPT NPE%

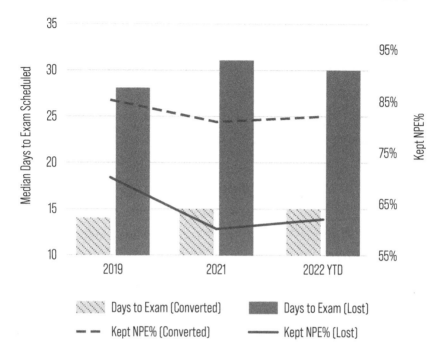

In the chart above, the left axis corresponds to the vertical bar chart. The striped bars show, by year, the average days between patient creation (when they called) to the NPE date for the converted patients, which ranges between twelve to fifteen days. The solid bars show the same for the patients who did not convert. Notice for the patients that did not convert, the average booking window in 2019 was a startlingly high twenty-seven days, balloons to as high as thirty-two days in 2021, and remains at thirty days in 2022 to date.

To validate the impact on the actual Kept NPE Rate, we plotted the rate for each group (measured using the horizontal lines, not the vertical bars) on the right axis. Both dashed and solid horizontal line groups show decay as days increase, but the solid line group delivers consistently lower Kept NPE Rate—starting out 10 points worse and increasing to a nearly 20-point gap. The reason for the widening gap is that the five-day increase in the booking window crossed a consumer behavior threshold of greater than a month. Those patients who are being given exam dates out over a month might schedule, but many of them are hanging up and immediately calling another practice to see if they can get in faster—or finding something else to do with their discretionary dollars while waiting for your exam slot to open up.

Needless to say, we suggest you become intentional about implementing a "culture of now" that assumes your patients want to start their treatment right away. Wouldn't you? It's far more convenient for patients to have their exam and start treatment during the same appointment, versus having to come back three or four times for unnecessary diagnostic and consultative appointments. Set expectations for an SDS, and be ready for it.

> *PATIENTS WHO ARE BEING GIVEN EXAM DATES OUT OVER A MONTH MIGHT SCHEDULE, BUT MANY OF THEM ARE HANGING UP AND IMMEDIATELY CALLING ANOTHER PRACTICE TO SEE IF THEY CAN GET IN FASTER.*

Same-day starts need to be the goal of every practice—to give every new patient the chance to start their new smile on day one. Of course, that's easy to say, but many patients miss out on that convenience because they're so focused on the price of treatment. Offering payment flexibility enables them to choose quality treatment they can afford, instead of missing out on treatment because of price.

The Power of Choice

As we mentioned previously, it's a big mistake to believe the myth that the only people who want, or need, low monthly payments are those with bad credit—or conversely, that people with good credit are fine with higher monthly payments. We've found many doctors still make that assumption, believing patients with good credit have more money to spend and are able (and willing) to make a bigger down payment and pay a higher amount monthly. To find out if that was actually true, we analyzed ortho industry numbers to answer three all-important questions:

- What happens when patients are allowed to choose from a virtually unlimited number of down payment and monthly payment options to customize their plan in a way that suits their individual financial needs?
- Which payment plan ($X down and $Y per month) do people choose most often when needing to finance their treatment?
- If we offer extended credit to all potential customers, how will their credit score impact how they choose to pay for treatment?

The data we gathered helped us answer those questions once and for all. When allowed to choose, we found that an average of 22 percent of all ortho patients selected to pay in full (PIF). We also discovered the optimal PIF discount to be 3 percent (higher discounts offered diminishing returns), but that practices could customize and adjust that discount percentage to control their cash flow as needed.

For the remainder of the patients who needed financing, we set about determining what payment options they preferred using our software's slider tool, which allowed prospective patients to design their own terms with full open choice. We first started by offering down payments as low as $250 and monthly payments extending out as long as thirty-six months to find out what our patients would prefer. We weren't sure what they'd choose, but the data soon made that clear.

Although the numbers proved that people with better credit do tend to put a little more money down, they also showed us that practices requiring $1,500 down payments for Invisalign (or other high-lab-fee technologies) were hampering their own growth. That conclusion was based on the fact that all credit groups chose down payments of $1,100 or less, with all but one group choosing down payments under $1,000. Although that's important to know, our most interesting takeaway had to do with monthly payments, dispelling the myth that people with better credit and higher income are willing to pay higher monthly rates. We were surprised to find the average patient preferred payments that fell between $185 and $205 per month, regardless of their FICO score, except for the very small number of people with sub-500 credit. So even though we found that patients with higher credit did translate to higher monthly choices (as you might expect), that difference was only $20 per month among patients with credit scores ranging from 500 to 900.

That preferred payment outcome surprised us as it was constant across such a wide disparity in credit scores. What this data shows is that the price of orthodontics is not infinitely elastic—meaning consumers believe orthodontic treatment should cost $200 or less a month, and charging more will cost you a lot of patient starts. If you think about it, you probably know quite a few families that are house and car rich but cash poor. Even high-income families with great credit have financial commitments and constraints (e.g., private school, music lessons, eTC:) that may leave them feeling overextended. They've undoubtedly got a variety of other financial commitments ranging from vacation houses and boats to private school tuition and investment programs.

PLANS CHOSEN BY CREDIT SCORE

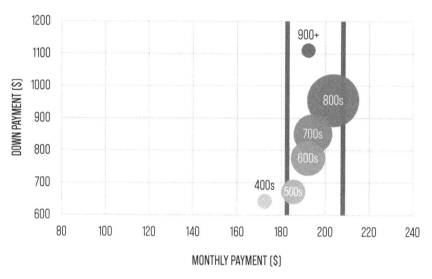

So the takeaway truth is that no matter what technology you use or how premium your treatment might be, you need to be able to price it around $200 per month, regardless of what income bracket you're serving. This conclusion, validated across over $5 billion in orthodontic production, reveals people from all walks of life, with all levels of income and creditworthiness, want (on average) orthodontic treatment to cost less than $1,000 down and $200 (or less) per month.

Of course, this finding begs the question of what to do about all the higher costs associated with the accelerated technology orthodontists now promote. Our data provided the answer and taught us an important lesson that may run counter to your current thinking: it's not only OK to allow payment beyond treatment, but it's also a must if you want your practice to grow. There. We said it. If you aren't offering flexible financing to allow for this range of payment options, it's likely you're causing a lot of patients to walk away. Once you reverse course and follow the data, you'll discover that open choice is the most effective way to ensure your patients permit you to start treatment.

Right about now, many are probably feeling nervous and thinking, "Extending terms can hurt my cash flow and increase patient default risk." Orthodontists have heard that for years and have been told that the antidote for such risk is to require higher down payments and shorter repayment times to "protect" themselves. "Protecting" yourself with minimum down payments starting in the $1,500 (and up) range will run off countless prospective patients who simply can't afford your terms.

IT'S NOT ONLY OK TO ALLOW PAYMENT BEYOND TREATMENT, BUT IT'S ALSO A MUST IF YOU WANT YOUR PRACTICE TO GROW.

Seen in that light, it should become crystal clear that the old, inflexible financing approach doesn't actually protect your practice from risk but "protects" it from growth. What will protect you is implementing a tight, consistent account-monitoring system at the same time you start allowing extended plans to stimulate growth. One key reason for this outcome is that encouraging patients to choose plans that fit comfortably within their budget encourages repayment. If they can comfortably afford to pay, they want to pay. Conversely, you might successfully convince a patient to stretch their monthly budget to fit your needs, but from that point on that patient is constantly running at or beyond their financial limit to where they either can't sustain that payment month after month, and any financial blip will tip them over to where they stop paying.

That being said, we want to suggest another way of thinking about establishing payment terms: stop treating it as a negotiation. As with your treatment plan, even a fee presentation can be considered a consultation and conducted as a consult with clinical benefit to your patients. You don't have to present options by saying something neutral and bland like, "Here are our standard choices—which one would you like?" Instead, you can confidently reassure and inspire patients by telling them, "We want to make sure you get the best treatment and payment option possible for you." Then hand the patient a tablet displaying a payment-option slider tool, and show them how to use it.

A team member's involvement is key here because the slider isn't some automatic technical gadget we started using to make our jobs easier, but a finely tuned, highly sophisticated, patient-facing, digital-consultation tool. That's why we don't recommend starting a financial presentation by simply handing off the tablet to patients and leaving them alone to pick whatever financing terms they want. You still need your TC to tout the value your practice offers and establish rapport with patients, and to show them how the flexible options work. If you can't come to a quick agreement, then you would turn the power of open choice over to the patient. The pressure release of being able to weigh their financial options without judgment or having to reveal their financial situation opens up opportunities for patients who are more guarded or less willing to actively negotiate. But once you start seeing the wide array of plans people pick from, you'll realize that even the best TC can't gauge patients' needs or size their wallets as well as they may think they can. In fact, data indicates that the average TC has what we call "hyperempathy," which just means that they assume many patients or families can't make larger down payments and unwittingly influence the size of the down payments lower than necessary. Although an excellently trained TC can accomplish something similar without it, a payment-option slider helps a less experienced TC perform at a productive level their first day on the job.

Letting your patients choose their own payment plans from the newly expanded array of options the slider provides feels reassuring and empowering to them. The reason this kind of slider works so well is that it allows patients to take control of their payment choices while selecting terms favorable to an office's cash flow. It's another win-win for both the patient and the practice. Although other companies have tried to play catch-up and have created sliders of their own, they don't work as well since they're missing many of the key components we built into OrthoFi's slider—including its presentation algorithm and the ability to charge interest.

In the next chapter, we'll discuss how intelligent flexibility can drive practice growth with open-choice concepts that increase your cash flow and leverage. What's leverage? It's the ability to use what you have and make it go further the way a crowbar can move a boulder by providing a multiplying force. We'll explore the topic of leverage itself and explain how you can start using it right away to help your business thrive.

Takeaways for Adding Flexibility

- There's no correlation between fee and conversion when ortho charges range from $5,300 to $7,000. People choose quality and affordability—not low price.
- Flexibility allows patients to choose quality over price. So don't protect yourself from growth.
- People will pay *more* in total to get affordable monthly payments (more on this later in the section on interest-bearing plans).
- The majority of your patients want down payments under $1,000 and monthly payment plans under $200. If you aren't offering these plans to *everyone*, you are leaking patients out of your intake funnel.

6

MAXIMIZE CASH FLOW/LEVERAGE

People tend to resist that which is forced upon them.
People tend to support that which they help to create.

—VINCE PFAFF

Orthodontists are seeing record numbers of adults seeking and starting orthodontic treatment in the United States and Canada. In 2021 alone, adults seeking treatment increased by 34 percent, and that trend shows no signs of slowing down, according to an American Association of Orthodontists "Economics of Orthodontics" survey. The convenience and cosmetic appeal of clear-aligner technology undoubtedly have a lot to do with that trend, and orthodontists are pleased to provide this popular treatment. But whether a new patient is a middle-aged software engineer or a preteen brought in by a parent, finding ways to accommodate the budgets of those prospective patients must be your highest priority if you want them to start treatment at your practice. The Federal Reserve has reported only 63 percent of consumers to have the cash or savings to handle an unexpected expense of $400 at any given time, making affordability of treatment crucial to anyone's success. When all these trends are considered, many orthodontists will see the looming problem: aligners are growing increasingly popular, but nearly half of all consumers won't be able to pay the high up-front lab fees most conventional orthodontic practices require to start treatment. That's where leveraging a smaller down payment and extending payment plans can save the day to win those patients and grow your practice.

I owe my knowledge of leverage to my coauthor, Oliver Gelles, and a few other very smart businesspeople. Thanks to industry experts like Oliver, I've come to understand how to apply the power of leverage to achieve impressive growth in my own orthodontic practice. To be completely honest, I do remember learning about levers exerting leverage in a physics class—but I had no idea how that term applied to managing my ortho practice, and there's a perfectly good reason for that: business training was completely absent from my orthodontic residency, and the subject never came up. And no one in orthodontics was using or teaching these concepts. That's too bad because running a successful practice in the real world requires not only clinical skills, but the knowledge of powerful business concepts such as leverage creation to compete with a growing number of DTC and other competitors. Many didn't even exist during my residency, but the growing amount of competitors in our space are here to stay, and they've changed the way we need to conduct business—using leverage.

Entrepreneur magazine describes leverage as "the key to making what you have go much further." Put another way, leverage can be defined as the advantageous condition of having a relatively small amount of cost yield a relatively high level of returns. The term can be used as a noun ("Leverage is a way to allow a business to expand") or as a verb ("Businesses leverage themselves by getting loans for expansion"). We'll talk about both types in this chapter and explain their respective benefits to practice growth.

Before we do, it's important to point out what a real practice growth killer it is to hold prospective patients hostage by demanding a high down payment before starting their treatment. I frequently hear doctors espouse this faulty approach. "I need to get X number of dollars up front to cover my lab costs before the patient can start," doctors tell me. And I know the people over at Invisalign hear the same thing until they're blue in the face! "What's the problem with that very traditional policy?" you ask. If you stop and think about it, the answer is obvious: the lab fees for many high-tech braces and custom wires are usually north of $1,000, and for aligners, it can be $1,800 or more. Since nearly half of your prospective patients don't have this kind of money at their disposal for a down payment, demanding it anyway blocks a large number of people from being able to afford starting treatment in your office.

Creating Leverage with Choice

Let's look at a better approach and start with what the data reveals about patient-selected down payment and monthly payment amounts. Each dot on the chart below illustrates the combination of monthly payments and down payments selected by a person who financed their treatment (payment in full was not included here). Overall, these dots reveal the surprisingly wide variety of plans people choose when given the freedom to pick the terms they prefer.

PATIENT PLANS SELECTED 2018-2022

[Excluding Pay-In-Full]

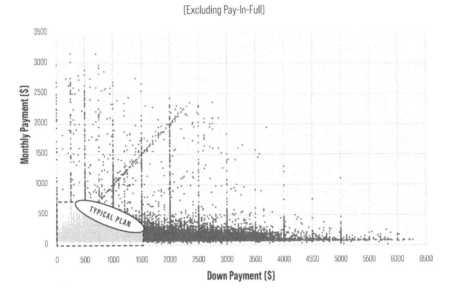

When you look closely, you'll see someone actually opted to pay $250 down and $740 per month, while another person selected $4,500 down and $50 per month! No practice normally offers those terms as one of their options, yet the chart clearly proves there are people who would choose those terms if they were given the choice to do so. Notice that the circled area represents the average range of financial terms the majority of practices offer their patients. When you look outside that small area, you'll also notice that 90 percent of the dots in the chart are lying outside the designated "typical plan" area. That obviously means "average" is not synonymous with "most," since the normal plans offered by orthodontists were just a small portion of other possible plans selected "most" by patients. In other words, when patients were allowed to select their own terms, the greatest number of plans patients chose were outside the limited area of normal plans offered by ortho practices.

Look again at the chart, and take note of the fact that it's mostly darker gray, except for the smaller, light gray area in the bottom left corner. That area denotes patients with payment terms nearly all orthodontists would consider unfavorable to their bottom line, whereas the darker gray area represents patients who chose terms nearly all orthodontists would deem favorable—plans with a higher down or a higher monthly that create a positive cash flow for the practice. Since the majority of payment plans are in the darker gray, "favorable" area, many doctors receive that surplus money and put it in their pocket and consider it theirs—even though they haven't completed, or even started, the patients' treatments yet. To be perfectly honest, orthodontists are usually very willing to accept money from people before doing any treatment, but get very nervous (or balk completely) at the idea of letting someone start treatment without covering their up-front costs. That may seem like Good Business 101, but it actually causes those practices to lose a lot of potential patients they could retain profitably. The solution to this dilemma is shockingly simple: rather than eliminate those people from your practice (i.e., lose their business), simply take some of the surplus money given to you by the patients in the darker gray area of the chart, and apply it to the lab bills for the people in the light gray area. Voilà! Leverage has been created to generate a higher number of new patient starts and your practice grows.

Now we realize many of you would rather stick with the "I need to cover my lab bill before allowing someone to start treatment" approach and keep operating your practice the old-school way you always have. But this outdated idea is actually foolish, shortsighted, and expensive (to you). The only thing you're doing by charging everyone a $1,500 down payment to begin treatment is stunting the growth potential of your practice and preventing you from earning additional business and profit. The smarter strategy would be to use the power of open choice to allow more affordable down payments and extended terms while using incentives to entice them to pay faster and pay more down if they can. Tiered discounts encourage higher down payments, and default risk is hedged by charging varying rates of interest depending on the length of payment plans and credit scores, where applicable.

This approach drives success so effectively, it's one of the primary reasons practices that start using OrthoFi average over 14 percent growth over prior years—growth generated by using the service to handle a much wider array of payment plan options for many additional patients. That statistic is not meant to be a sales pitch for OrthoFi but rather is a great example of how creating leverage—rather than creating an insurmountable down payment for patients—is the key to making what you're already doing more profitable. *Entrepreneur* magazine, as well as every savvy businessperson, knows this already. The Association of Dental Support Organizations knows it as well, which is exactly why they promote advertising based on very flexible payment terms for orthodontic services. It's time for orthodontists to utilize this same leverage before their restrictive terms drive patients away from where they belong—in the hands of a highly skilled orthodontic specialist. Now that you've seen the numbers for yourself, we'll provide further details on how to access your new, untapped patient group by leveraging patient choice and cash flow to grow your practice.

> PRACTICES THAT START USING ORTHOFI AVERAGE OVER 14 PERCENT GROWTH OVER PRIOR YEARS.

Assessing Current Cash Flow

Before tackling the topic of cash-flow management, it's important to emphasize that orthodontists, in general, don't manage their cash flow very well. Instead, far too many doctors practice what we call "lemonade stand" cash management. If you're one of them, you sell your "lemonade" (braces), collect money, pay bills, and smilingly shake the cash box on your way out to spend what's left over. But "real" businesses understand the reality of seasonal swings and strategically budget the amount of operating profit they spend over time. In addition, they periodically (semiannually, rather than monthly or weekly) bonus the extra earnings into a reserve cash fund. Only when the reserve cash fund becomes large enough to cover several months' expenses do they sweep the leftover cash into the profit bucket. Applying this approach is essential in a growing business, as expenses can outpace intake during periods of rapid growth and cash reserves are necessary to make rapid growth manageable.

You'll need to adopt this same cash-management approach to reap the benefits of intelligent flexibility and leverage to grow your practice. But before you start implementing these measures, it's important to first assess your current cash-flow situation. What we mean is this: once you shift away from requiring a $1,000 to $1,500 down payment from every patient—to allowing the kind of flexible payment options we recommend—your cash flow will temporarily tighten up, no matter how smart you are with your cash flow. But stay the course! Initiating payment flexibility will pay significant dividends and reward you with practice growth that will translate to much more revenue and profit in the long run.

Just remember, starting out, you need to consider your short-term cash reserves and be sure to build up extra reserves to compensate for the inevitable first few months of growth-related cash depletion. You may not want to go to this length, but many businesses with high margins, like orthodontic practices, use short-term lines of credit to infuse cash to fuel growth. It's certainly worth considering. In my own practice, I used to think having to access a line of credit was the result of cash-management failure, but I now realize it's a smart business tactic when it's used to fuel rapid growth and then paid back quickly as cash flow catches up to production.

Which Flow—Transactional or Aggregate?

In a perfect world, all of your patients would pay in full before treatment, thereby eliminating the need for your office to finance receivables altogether. Orthodontists would simply need to manage their savings (as discussed above) to allow the business to cover expenses during the leaner months that recur on a seasonal basis. But we don't live in that perfect kind of world, and the majority of your orthodontic clientele cannot afford to pay in full—requiring orthodontists to provide financing. When structuring that financing, you have two approaches to consider: transactional cash-flow management and aggregate cash-flow management. Both of these approaches will allow appropriate cash flow, but only one will simultaneously create the leverage we've been discussing in this chapter.

Transactional cash-flow management involves evaluating every single financial transaction in a vacuum and determining the cash-flow requirements for the office based on that one transaction. For example, if the patient wants clear aligners, you would need to collect, at minimum, the lab fee up front to avoid being cash-flow negative on that particular transaction. This is the most common modality for cash-flow management in orthodontics. Although transactional management is much simpler, the data makes it clear that transactional management is also the single biggest impediment to growth in orthodontics today.

Aggregate cash-flow management is the alternative strategy we recommend that allows you to intelligently create leverage in your business while setting a healthy and consistent cash flow. It does not consider each individual transaction but rather the blended consequences of all total transactions. Using this method permits you to offer payment flexibility to those who need it—and more importantly, to those who would not start treatment without it—while still enticing those who can afford to pay extra up front to do so more often. Instead of managing individual transactions, you will monitor key performance indicators (KPIs) that show you the state of your aggregate cash-flow situation at any given time so you can manage your cash accordingly.

Open Choice Ensures a Healthy Aggregate Balance

If you look back at the payment plan chart we showed you earlier, you'll see the vast majority of dots (representing individual payment plans) extend far outside the small circled area in light gray that denotes the average of plans offered around the country. Yes, some dots clearly show lower down payments and monthly payment selections, but a significant number are higher on both ends, meaning they'll produce positive cash flow. As you keep that in mind, consider the fact that most offices offer a discount for paying in full (PIF), which entices at least 20 percent of their patients to pay this way. Additionally, 15 to 20 percent of an office's cash flow comes from down payments, and the rest is accounted for with insurance payments and monthly payments. But there's simply no good reason to limit yourself to this kind of restrictive, binary choice of offering either pay-in-full or one option for financing over time.

As you may be aware, very few practices ever get 75 percent or 50 percent down because few patients have any incentive to do so, and very few TCs even consider asking for that high of a down payment. But you can easily create such motivation with tiered down payment incentives that scale higher with larger down payments. If you offer a 5 percent PIF discount, for example, you can also add a 3 percent and a 2 percent incentive tier for 75 percent and 50 percent down payments, respectively. This strategy has proven very effective at stimulating more patients to pick higher down payment options. Across a sample of 130 OrthoFi practices over an eighteen-month period, 24 percent of cases pay in full, and the average down payment on the rest is $834, even though the vast majority of patients had the choice to put as little as $250 down! When all these choices are blended together, the average initial payment per case is $1,354—plenty of cash flow to run a growing practice.

Regarding monthlies, a similar smart strategy can be employed to financially incentivize patients to pick plans of shorter duration. Doing so simply requires disincentivizing patients to pick extended payment plan options unless they really have to. As of today, most practices aren't leveraging the power of charging interest on payment terms, even when those terms extend months past the completion of treatment.

That's a mistake and here's why: offering flexibility in your payment options is certainly a good way to grow your practice, but offering extended plan options to your patients that charge 0 percent interest is not. Having no disincentive for extended terms encourages more patients to choose that option—something that will hurt your cash flow overall. But adding a modest amount of interest to extended financing plans helps you avoid those cash-flow problems by incentivizing patients to choose shorter plans while not being overly punitive to those who need extended plans. Again, you're not forcing them into shorter plans. You're incentivizing them to choose shorter plans. So those who need lower monthly payments have a way to start with you, and those who don't will choose the shorter plans you want. The combination of these two tactics—tiered discounts for varying down payment amounts and charging varying interest rates based on plan length—yields a much wider scatter of plan choices (both on the high and low end) to create an aggregate cash flow that is sustainable while allowing flexibility to those that need it.

Is It Working Yet?

Adopting an aggregate cash-flow model may seem like a leap of faith, as a gamble of sorts, which bets all the "dots" will come together in a way that collectively balances out. But you may be relieved to know we're not advocating that kind of "Close your eyes and jump" mentality. Instead, we're advising you to develop and monitor a set of metrics that will reveal what's actually happening to your inflow and outflow of cash. That way, you can adjust where needed, when your cash flow is off the mark. To that end, it's critical to stay on top of monthly and yearly KPIs to track your cash flow. Two critical KPIs you need to track to manage cash flow are same-day cash and payment percentage of treatment length.

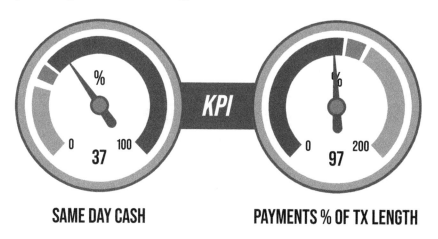

SAME DAY CASH   PAYMENTS % OF TX LENGTH

Same-day cash (SDC) is the first KPI metric you'll need to monitor. To calculate your SDC, you find the sum of the total, the combined amount of money your practice receives daily from pay-in-full (PIF) patients and down payments (DPs), then divide it by the cost of their overall treatment expressed as total patient responsibility (TPR). (TPR may also express the entire cost of a patient's treatment minus the value of their insurance benefit if they have any.)

So the SDC = (PIF + DP)/TPR.

If 20 percent of your patients pay in full, for example (we recommend aiming for this), of the remaining 80 percent of your TPR receivables, approximately 17 percent of it should be collected as a down payment (17 percent of 80 percent is 14 percent). So if you add 20 percent of those patients who "pay in full" to the 14 percent coming from down payments, your SDC should equal approximately 34 percent of your total patient receivables on any given day.

Once you're able to monitor this powerful SDC metric, you can correctly manage your aggregate cash flow. When you have a month with an SDC percentage higher than your target, you need to reinvest the extra cash flow to balance out the months with fewer pay-in-fulls or lower downs (instead of taking that extra money out of the "lemonade stand register"). Over time, using this kind of aggregate cash-flow management will increase and compound your volume of same-day cash dollars in a way that will yield a very nice six-month, or annual, bonus for you.

Payment percentage of treatment length (PTL) is the second KPI metric you'll want to track. It monitors how closely the average term of financing you offer aligns to your patients' average estimated length of treatment. In my own practice, for example, we use many systems to facilitate shorter treatment times (my office averages sixteen months across all full-treatment patients), so our PTL reflects how close the average payment term is to that sixteen months. This allows us to manage risk appropriately by only allowing extended terms to those who really need them. In doing so, we avoid an increase in aggregate risk and the front office burden created by adding a large chunk of overall patients who have opted for long-term payment financing. And that's how you intelligently create leverage to scale your business without becoming overly cash poor in the process.

Open Choice Is the New Gold Standard for Payments

Just to review, most practices only offer a discount for patients who can pay in full. This gets about 20 percent of new patients to go that route. But the rest of their patients have no incentive to choose a substantial down payment. Since the majority of these practices offer no other discounts and don't generally charge any kind of interest (even for patients who end up finishing their payments posttreatment), patients are given no financial incentive and no risk.

That's why tiered down payment incentives are part of the new gold standard we recommend. To start, we advise offering a 5 percent discount for patients who can pay in full, and smaller incentives for those who can pay 50 percent or 75 percent down. In addition, it's important to provide patients with more payment options, using an open-choice payment slider on a tablet patients can use to customize their down payment and their monthly payment into a flexible (but secure) payment option of their choice. What that data verifies is something we've long suspected—that customization is the future of collecting payments, and we've already seen this kind of system repeatedly achieve a 98 percent collection rate or better. This combination of payment solutions creates a proven system of aggregate cash-flow management, which not only sustains a practice but also keeps it growing—especially when your practice handles collections professionally and honestly. When you're managing in this aggregate manner, it means your practice will see an eventual increase in same-day cash and overall collections.

The hard data we've shared should be proof enough to convince you that financial flexibility will grow your business and won't preclude good collections. But there's another metric you'll need to understand: a measurement called the variable contribution margin (VCM). Never heard of it? It's the "margin" that results when your practice's variable production costs are subtracted from its revenue. And the surprising truth is that keeping track of this measurement will help protect your bottom line as nothing else can. In the upcoming chapter, we're going to clue you in on how to calculate your VCM and show you how to use your knowledge of that margin to confidently switch your practice into growth mode.

Takeaways for Cash Flow/Leverage

- Don't require a $1,500 down payment to begin treatment. It stunts the growth potential of your practice and prevents you from earning more business from the growing number of patients wanting clear aligners.
- Allow lower down payments and extended terms, then charge interest where applicable to hedge your default risk. Leveraging *smaller* down payments and *longer* payment plans is like applying a crowbar to raise your production.
- Manage risk appropriately by only offering extended terms to those who really need it, and don't be afraid to charge interest to create a disincentive.

- Adopt the strategy of aggregate cash-flow management to establish a healthy and consistent cash flow, then use your total combined transactions to leverage practice growth.

7

SAFER RISK MANAGEMENT

The biggest risk is not taking any risk ... In a world
that's changing really quickly, the only strategy
that is guaranteed to fail is not taking risks.

—MARK ZUCKERBERG

"Flexible financing sounds great, but do people actually pay?" That's one of the questions we hear most often, and it's a perfectly legitimate concern, considering how we've all been taught to think about financing risk in the past (i.e., it's risky!). But we can assure you: "Yes, people do pay when offered flexible financing. And the hard data gleaned from several billion dollars in receivables proves it."

Harnessing the power of leverage and cash flow really does allow you to be ultra-flexible with your financial terms—while still maintaining the healthy aggregate cash flow you need to pay your bills as your practice grows. Still not convinced? You're probably not alone. Orthodontists tend to have a hyperdetailed memory of that one patient (several years ago) who didn't pay enough before defaulting to cover their Invisalign lab bill. Even though such incidents are rare, many doctors still view their patients with suspicion, and it shapes their risk-management approach in a way that hurts their practice's potential for growth. They develop practice systems that are highly restrictive based on the behavior of the few and not the vast majority. Viewing people through a lens of doubt has led to an insidious, specialty-wide brain freeze about how to best appeal to prospective patients. This attitude of suspicion has also contributed to the rapid rise of competitors.

A lot of these competitors are run by executives with big-business experience—CEOs who have long advocated using the more innovative and lucrative approach to patient financing we've been recommending in this book. Frankly, in retrospect, most orthodontists have been very slow to understand and apply these business strategies for two very good reasons: first, they weren't offered business-management training during residency, and second, their lack of competitors in the past didn't compel them to acquire that training or innovate. That's no longer the case! Now it's absolutely essential to know how to manage risk effectively and understand and apply good business development principles such as flexible financing, aggregate cash flow, and variable contribution margin (VCM).

VCM: The Most Important Number You Don't Know

Previously, we defined VCM as the remaining money left over after your practice's variable production costs are subtracted from its sales revenue.

VCM = REVENUE - VARIABLE PRODUCTION COSTS

The difference that results is a dollar amount that can be used to cover fixed costs (such as payroll, rent, and utilities), and once those costs are covered, any excess can be considered earnings. If you expect your practice to thrive amid the growing competition for patients, you'll need to monitor your VCM to know how to apply your receivables to grow your business. With that goal in mind, we want to help you understand your VCM better by defining the two basic types of expenses orthodontists incur in their practices daily: fixed costs and variable costs.

Fixed costs are the expenses associated with running a business that do not change with your level of productivity. Rent, office salaries, utilities, and cable are all examples of costs that remain stable, or relatively stable, regardless of the number of patients you start. Once you experience significant growth, it will be necessary to add fixed costs by hiring another employee or moving to a bigger space; however, these costs do not change on a start-by-start basis. Your phone bill does not go up or down if you start a new patient.

Variable costs, on the other hand, are the expenses that do change, depending on how many patients you start. If you start another Invisalign case, for instance, you will owe another lab bill, plus the cost of glue for the attachments, a special aligner bag, extra tray covers, and the swag you give to each new patient starting treatment, eTC: These costs only occur when someone starts and don't exist if someone doesn't start.

As you probably already know, your overhead is the total expense of running your practice, and it's a combination of both the fixed and the variable costs you incur to keep your doors open and your patients smiling. For basic accounting purposes, your overhead is calculated with the following simple equation:

FIXED COSTS + VARIABLE COSTS = PRACTICE OVERHEAD

When considering the fixed, versus variable, type of expenses in an orthodontic practice, the amount you spend each month on fixed costs is going to be much larger than your variable costs. That's because the largest fixed expense in any orthodontic office involves payroll. But once payroll and other fixed overhead are paid, the remainder of your expenses are going to be variable ones—related to the specific costs of each new patient starting treatment. At some point, your fixed costs will be paid for, but your capacity to treat additional patients will remain open. So once you achieve a certain amount of production (specific to each practice), you'll have no more fixed costs to pay when you start an additional patient.

All revenue produced after that point will be subject to the VCM, which will continue to grow bigger until you reach the volume of new patient starts that requires you to hire additional staff or grow your footprint with a bigger facility. Since practices typically have up to 20 percent open capacity, this means you can treat 20 percent additional patients while only incurring smaller, variable, and incremental costs. As an example, let's consider an office with 60 percent overhead expenses and an average treatment fee of $5,000. Even if the doctor used "expensive" braces and wires, the incremental cost is still relatively low, compared to covering the remaining expense in the fixed category as shown:

- **Fixed costs:** Rent, salaries, phone, utilities, cable, computers, lawn care: $2,300 (46 percent)
- **Variable costs:** Self-ligating braces, adhesive, wires, and patient perks: $700 (14 percent)

Using the cost breakdown above, each additional patient costs only $700, yielding an 86 percent VCM. Typical clear-aligner treatment with Invisalign, Spark, Clarity, eTC:, yields slightly less, or around 70 percent VCM, because the variable expense of lab fees is higher. Even so, patients you treat "on top of" your existing volume are extremely profitable. This is why collections and receivables data demonstrates you can gain millions in profitability while risking an overall default rate well below 2 percent by offering flexible financing.

Let's assume, for example, you start using our recommended flexible financing approach right away but only gain new patient starts from those choosing riskier extended financing plans. Out of the first nearly 40,000 active plans managed through OrthoFi, 10,833 patients chose terms longer than twenty-five months (representing $60.8 million in production). Does that scenario scare you? It shouldn't, and here's why.

> *COLLECTIONS AND RECEIVABLES DATA DEMONSTRATES YOU CAN GAIN MILLIONS IN PROFITABILITY WHILE RISKING AN OVERALL DEFAULT RATE WELL BELOW 2 PERCENT BY OFFERING FLEXIBLE FINANCING.*

If you view OrthoFi practices and the collective data it generates as one big practice instead of many small ones, that data suggests much of that $60.8 million of financed production for extended plans was incremental. Even if only half of these plans were incremental, that means that over $30 million came from starts most practices wouldn't have converted with more traditional higher down payments and fixed-monthly financing terms anyway. With that in mind, here's how those starts panned out after the twenty-five-month term ended.

- Net default impact percentage for plans over twenty-five months = 1.3 percent
- Overall rate of default across all plans = 0.7 percent
- Increased default risk from extended plans versus overall plans is 1.3 percent - 0.7 percent = 0.6 percent.

- Multiplying the $60,800,000 times the increased risk of 0.6 percent yields a comparatively low number: 60,800,000 x 0.6 percent = $364,800.

What do these numbers tell you? They show the business gained $30 million in additional revenue by only risking an additional $364,000 in default. Since this revenue stream was likely incremental, that means it was revenue gained on top of standard revenue and subject to incremental costs only (as fixed costs have already been paid by the business's other production). Assuming a 70 percent variable margin (that conservatively assumes a 28 percent Invisalign mix in your practice), the $364,000 in risk gained an extra $21 million in profit.

> ADDING INCREMENTAL STARTS BY BECOMING FLEXIBLE WITH YOUR PAYMENT PLANS IS LIKELY THE SMARTEST AND MOST LUCRATIVE THING YOU COULD POSSIBLY DO FOR YOUR BUSINESS.

Not a bad bet, right? Making the math small again to relate to an individual practice, let's subtract a couple of decimal points off the above numbers. Would you welcome an additional $210,000 in net income (even if it meant losing $3,640 to default) that left you with $206,360 in net profit? Of course you would! Even if our math was off by 500 percent, would you still risk $3,640 to gain $103,180? We think it's safe to assume everyone would be confident about making that bet all day long and twice on Sundays.

So the moral of the math is that adding incremental starts by becoming flexible with your payment plans—even if they are "riskier" plans—is likely the smartest and most lucrative thing you could possibly do for your business. Besides the profitability of this approach, you have a social obligation to provide excellent care to those who can't afford traditional terms anyway, so it's a win-win situation, which we all know is the best kind!

What It Takes to Collect on Flexibility

Despite the immense profitability of financing flexibility, it's still smart to use savvy risk-management strategies to minimize any potential for loss. Extended terms can certainly cause cash-flow problems and increase the likelihood that patients will default if you don't have an effective plan in place to reduce those outcomes. Hopefully, the kind of plan that springs to mind isn't the outmoded orthodontist's antidote for "risky" patients—high monthly payments and down payments north of $1,500—to "protect" yourself from risk. As we've pointed out previously, that risk mitigation approach works really well at running off countless patients who can't afford such terms.

As an alternative, it makes a lot of sense to start doing what every other savvy business does: simply charge interest to hedge the risk of extending payments.

"Whoa! Isn't that some kind of industry heresy?" you ask. "And would orthodontic patients really be willing to pay interest for their treatments?"

Many industry traditionalists didn't think so, but we disagreed, knowing a certain percentage of patients already pay interest for pretty much everything else they buy. Why would our industry be any different? We're happy to report our logic was correct, and here's the data to prove it:

Across over $5 billion of production, we found on average 9.5 percent of all patients elected to pay interest, while in some offices, the percentage of patients who chose interest-bearing accounts was closer to 15 percent. I think most people—including us—anticipated only the "risky" patients would choose interest-bearing payment plans. Wanting to confirm that, we looked at the distribution of people selecting those plans for each credit score level. As expected, we found the highest distribution of people selecting interest-bearing payment plans were people with lower credit scores. But we were surprised to see a very significant portion of people with good or very good credit still selected interest-bearing plans.

We found that (depending on the demographics of your office's location) between 6 and 12 percent of people will choose to pay interest in exchange for the affordability of an extended payment plan. Of course, the amount of interest charged will make a difference to consumers who might be put off by the high-interest rates charged by some credit cards or other lending services.

FINANCED PAYMENT PLANS

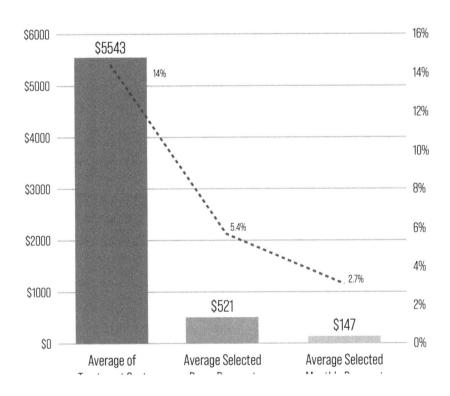

The previous chart displays the distribution of people who chose interest-bearing payment plans, and it suggests three interesting takeaways:

1. The total cost of treatment was $5,543, which is about $500 *more expensive* than the average cost of treatment across OrthoFi practices.
2. The average down payment selected was just over $500.
3. The average monthly payment was about $150.

The chart clearly shows people are willing to pay higher prices for your services if you make it affordable for them, indicating there is a subset of patients who will do so if you offer those services for $500 down and $150 per month.

Many people wonder why the interest rate isn't above 20 percent, as it is for credit cards, but the reason is simple: lenders typically make money off lending money and therefore need to charge much larger interest rates to cover their default risk. If you think about it, lenders lose money until they recover every penny they have loaned. The way they earn money is by charging interest and fees. Orthodontists, on the other hand, make money in an industry where the default risk is much lower and they only need to cover their costs to begin making money, and not after recovering their full fee. That means orthodontists only need to charge interest for two reasons:

1. A disincentive for people who can afford shorter payment plans—and corresponding higher monthly payments—to shorten their terms to both mitigate your risk and help your cash flow.
2. A hedge against the additional risk taken on by accepting the longer payment plans. The interest income earned will offset some of the higher defaults.

Because the VCM for treating these cases is so high, you want to treat as many of them as possible. If you applied a significantly higher interest rate, you would decrease your conversion percentage. The offsetting loss of revenue would never be made up by charging higher interest fees. So, unlike the banks, you don't need to recover the full cost of treatment plus interest to be profitable. You only need to cover your variable expenses (often 15 percent of the fee or lower) in order to become profitable. Being a lender or being a doctor are very different sides of the same coin when it comes to how profiting from orthodontic plans is achieved.

What conclusions can we offer from this data? First, people will willingly pay you more total money for better quality orthodontic treatment if you allow them to make a lower down payment and a lower monthly payment, over the course of a longer repayment plan. Second, about 10 percent of all patients need a monthly payment of $150. Third, a large number of the patients who do need the lower payments and extended terms have good or very good credit, despite the fact that having good credit and "can't afford over $150 per month" seem contradictory.

With all that in mind, you'll find it reassuring that OrthoFi's collections data shows 98 percent of all patients processed through the system to date don't default. So managing risk by using interest— rather than prohibitive down payments or monthly payments—is smart and profitable, both in terms of the interest income generated and driving up orthodontic case starts.

Accounts Receivables (AR) Systems

At a time when the orthodontic industry is changing so rapidly, doing things "like you've always done them" is going to result in stasis or decline, instead of growth. In order to keep growing, you're going to need to operate out of a new financial management paradigm that requires you to become extremely flexible with your patients' down payments and monthly payments—offering extended payment terms well beyond the estimated length of treatment. These proven principles need to shape the way you offer financing in your office.

When we first started shaking things up with these new-fangled notions, orthodontic traditionalists called our ideas "dangerous" and warned us that our financial principles were "a recipe for disaster." They were wrong. Despite the "disaster" predicted by these industry voices of doom, we've seen rapid growth and an industry-leading solid percentage. We've disproven the false notion (once and for all) that allowing payment terms beyond treatment time is bad for business. Industry dogma will try to convince you that 50 percent of "non A" patients won't pay or prove profitable, and you shouldn't seek them as patients. Again, fake news.

Historically, for example, the industry gold standard for collections has been 3 percent past thirty days' delinquency, with a 1 to 1.5 percent default rate. But when we used our software to test these traditional risk-management principles across all markets, we proved these legacy standards were so outdated and obsolete that they actually restricted

COMPLETE PLAN COLLECTION SUMMARY			
# Default Accounts	% Default Accounts	$ Default	Default Rate ($)
165	1.8%	$264K	0.7%

business success. We verified that growth in the new orthodontic market is going to require following a new gold standard of financial principles. We're going to explain two of those new financial principles right now.

Financial Principle 1: Offering a Wide Range of Flexible Terms Doesn't Have to Compromise Your Collection Rate

In today's market and economic environment, flexibility around your payment options is a must-have. Solid data proves you'll stimulate practice growth by offering truly open choice that allows people to control their own terms. Although adopting this new approach may feel like you're giving up your control over securing payment for treatment, that's not the case. But we know that's why so many of you have asked how flexibility impacts collections. So let's reference the numbers from the first 40,000 individual payment plans and over $125,000,000 in patient receivables processed, and let those numbers speak for themselves. Of that production total, 9,274 of those plans have been paid off or have reached term and should have been paid ($37,800,000 in production). In the following collection summary chart, the data shows the percentage of default still remains very low, despite what would previously be considered "risky" financial principles.

> DEFAULTS THAT PAY ENOUGH TO COVER MOST, OR ALL, OF THE EXPENSES ASSOCIATED WITH PROVIDED TREATMENT, FOR EXAMPLE, MEAN LOSS OF PROFITABILITY BUT NOT LOSS OF MONEY.

For this discussion, keep in mind that we're considering amounts beyond 180 days as projected default. The industry average is around 1.5 percent, and the gold standard has historically been 1 percent. To clarify, "default" is not synonymous with "has paid nothing." Also, "default" is a broad category that does not take into account whether a patient stopped paying toward the beginning or toward the end of their repayment plan. That's an important distinction since it obviously impacts the amount of loss incurred by a practice. Defaults that pay enough to cover most, or all, of the expenses associated with provided treatment, for example, mean loss of profitability but not loss of money.

The "timing of default" graph below shows at what point along the payment plan the patient stopped paying. The Y-axis shows the number of default plans, and the X-axis shows at what point during the estimated treatment time the payment plan went into default. The dashed line depicts the dollar amount written off at each stage of treatment. If the original estimated treatment time was eighteen months, for example, and a patient stopped paying for nine months, the default would appear in the 50 percent bar since they stopped paying halfway through treatment.

TIMING OF DEFAULT AS % OF Tx TIME

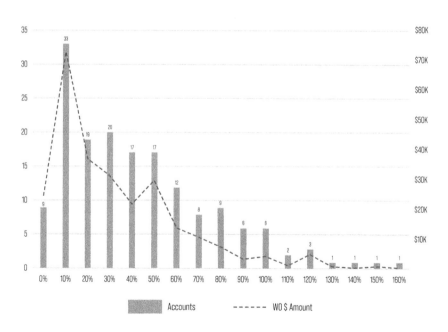

So the idea of limiting payment time to treatment time does not buy you much in the way of added security. It only serves to limit your appeal among prospective patients. Now if you tell people their treatment will take eighteen months, and it actually takes you twenty-four months or more, you may see an increase in default toward the tail end of their treatment. But that's a different statistical issue, signaling you have a clinical efficiency and treatment planning problem, which is too broad for the scope of this book. Keep in mind, however, that $2,400 per patient is still collected (on average) from patients that eventually default. Assuming a $5,000 average fee and a 50 percent operating margin, these default cases nearly break even, meaning that the average default case scenario isn't a true loss. You just don't make money on those few exceptions.

Financial Principle 2: If Managed Properly, Higher-Risk Plans and Patients Are Still Profitable

Of the nearly 40,000 active OrthoFi plans we studied, 10,833 were for terms longer than 25 months (representing $60,800,000 in production). At first glance, their default rate is noticeably higher than shorter payment terms. However, when you consider the interest income gained from these plans, the total default is substantially decreased.

This default rate chart shows a $1.6 million gross default, which is 2.7 percent of the total production for that group. To mitigate this loss, our software applies a low-interest rate for extended plans that offsets the incremental risk and splits the interest income with the practice. So when you add back the $786,000 interest that was earned by practices for those plans, the net default is cut nearly in half to $814,000. This yields a 1.3

COMPLETE PLAN COLLECTION SUMMARY			
# Default Accounts	% Default Accounts	$ Default	Default Rate ($)
418	3.8%	$1.6M	2.7%
- Interest Earned = $786K			
Net Default Impact = $814K			1.3%

percent default for the extended plans, and that percentage gets us within the industry's average default range, even for these most aggressive plans. So that's hardly a significant enough "risk" to avoid treating these patients. Besides, "riskier" patients are probably incremental to the volume you're doing now, which means you're yielding a much higher VCM on those cases anyway.

When blended across all payment plans, the default percentage we see is still just 1.9 percent, which is below the gold standard and 38 percent below the US practice median and inclusive of the new extended plans you might consider "risky." This data shows that extended plans won't hurt your overall collection rate when they're properly managed but will likely improve it instead.

> Everyone wants to grow, but not everyone is ready to grow. The data clearly shows that being accessible, persistent, and flexible with patients can—and will—get you more starts.

How to Calculate Your Receivables

We're often asked how to properly calculate receivables by orthodontists who are understandably confused by the process and are worried they're doing it wrong. Those doctors aren't lacking in financial smarts, they just received little business training and have to learn as they go. So we're going to help remedy that now by breaking down the subject of calculating receivables. We'll start by defining key terms and by providing a summary of how we perform receivables calculations, then clarifying what metrics you should be looking at to expertly manage your own practice's receivables. Although this can be pretty dry stuff, it's absolutely essential information for orthodontists trying to properly manage their businesses. Let's zero in on key terms you need to know first:

Same-day cash refers to a combination of payments received at the beginning of treatment from down payments (DP) and from patients who pay in full (PIF). It's important to monitor this ratio since knowing your same-day cash (SDC) percentage will be what allows you to manage your cash flow, while still allowing patients the choice of flexible payment terms. SDC payments are expressed as this equation:

$$SDC = (PIF + DP)/TPR$$

Receivable is a term Investopedia defines as "an asset designation applicable to all debts, unsettled transactions, or other monetary obligations owed to a company by its debtors or customers." Receivables are recorded by a company's accountants and reported on the balance sheet, and they include all debts owed to the company, even if the debts are not currently due. In orthodontics, moneys owed after SDC is collected are a blend of "accounts receivable" and "contracts receivable"—although we typically (and errantly) define our receivables as "accounts receivable" only.

Account receivable denotes the outstanding invoices a company has or the money the company is owed from its clients, in the present period. This term refers to the accounts a business has a right to receive because it has already delivered a product or service. In orthodontics, that obviously pertains to the portion of treatment you've already performed or an appliance you've already delivered but have not yet been paid for. Delivering a new retainer to a patient who hasn't paid for it yet or completing a percentage of a patient's treatment without having collected any payment for that partial treatment are two such examples. Historically, though, orthodontic practices operate with few true accounts receivable, as it was rare for the orthodontist to deliver significant portions of treatment without being paid for it, and offices routinely required any balances to be paid before removing braces.

Contract receivable is an amount expected to be realized in future periods for services you haven't yet rendered. In orthodontics, doctors typically bill for services before they're performed, but any portion of treatment that's yet to be done, and yet to be paid for, would be a contract receivable. Orthodontists have operated with very few true account receivable items in the past because doctors were advised (wrongly) to never take the braces off their patients before they'd fully paid off their account.

That "pay or else" approach is just the opposite of the one used by a furniture store, which will sell, finance, and deliver a couch many months or years before the couch is fully paid off. From the data we've gathered and analyzed, we now know the furniture store got it right, and their business strategy is one you'll have to adopt if you hope to remain competitive in today's marketplace.

There's just no avoiding it: orthodontists must become more flexible in their financial policies and, when necessary, extend terms to patients beyond their treatment time to allow lower monthly and down payments to those who need them. Of course, this approach will increase the number of true accounts receivable they manage, but the data confirms, if done properly, they'll incur little incremental financial risk in doing so. Since orthodontists don't ask or expect all of their patients to pay

THERE'S JUST NO AVOIDING IT: ORTHODONTISTS MUST BECOME MORE FLEXIBLE IN THEIR FINANCIAL POLICIES.

in full, they already have to actively and separately manage two kinds of contract receivables: first, those from patients, and, second, those from insurance companies.

Patient receivables are the total uncollected dollars owed to the practice by patients (excluding insurance), and they're created when doctors offer people the ability to make monthly payments. These patient receivables can be stated as an equation:

PATIENT RECEIVABLES = PRODUCTION - SDC - INSURANCE RECEIVABLES

Insurance receivables are those uncollected dollars owed to the practice by the patient via their insurance. The gold standard for insurance receivables is that 1 percent of your total AR should be past due (more than thirty days) insurance AR. As insurance AR is approximately 20 percent of the total AR in the average practice, this translates to about 5 percent of your total insurance AR. What many don't know is that there are a shocking number of times insurance companies fail to pay as scheduled—a scenario requiring your team to maintain active and diligent monitoring of all insurance receivables owed to your practice. Although management discussions in orthodontics typically revolve around the topic of patient receivables, it's very common to have a high delinquency rate of insurance receivables as well. Insurance companies much prefer insurance dollars to reside in their bank accounts and not yours. Since that's the case, your team is better able to pry those dollars out than your patients. That's why we strongly advise you to accept the assignment of insurance benefits and manage these receivables on behalf of your patients. Refusing to do so is tantamount to "not taking my insurance" to a lot of patients and will give your competitors who do accept assignment of benefit a competitive edge over your practice. (Note: As insurance companies continue to manage down the amount they reimburse, we may change this recommendation; however, as of the writing of this book, we still continue to recommend participating in non-DHMO plans.) These insurance receivables can be expressed as the following equation:

INSURANCE RECEIVABLES = PRODUCTION - SDC - PATIENT RECEIVABLES

Thirty- / sixty- / ninety-day receivables are typically those accounts receivable tracked by what is called an "aging" report that indicates how "old" receivables are and how long the patient has owed money they've not yet paid. Accounts under thirty days delinquent are typically not considered in a delinquency calculation, as the industry standard considers only moneys over thirty days unpaid to be delinquent. As an account ages, most know it becomes less and less likely it will be converted from a contract receivable to cash (i.e., less likely you will get paid).

TIER	CURRENT BALANCE	0-10 DAYS	11-30 DAYS	31-60 DAYS	61-90 DAYS	> 90 DAYS	TOTAL	%
1	$1,062,419.94	$739.68	$2,231.11	$719.46	$609.18	$3,398.00	$1,070,117.37	35.82%
2	$628,414.31	$1,131.66	$1,165.88	$596.19	$0.18	$2,708.05	$634,016.27	21.22%
3	$583,197.00	$3,320.50	$4,323.42	$4,308.20	$3,120.54	$18,653.34	$616,923.00	20.65%
4	$127,434.46	$1,191.38	$1,118.31	$1,634.42	$1,030.02	$3,409.72	$135,818.31	4.55%
5	$0.00	$0.00	$0.00	$0.00	$0.00	$0.00	$0.00	0.00%
6	$0.00	$0.00	$0.00	$0.00	$0.00	$0.00	$0.00	0.00%
No Check	$523,294.71	$1,092.44	$1,109.59	1,277.88	$767.29	$3,437.30	$530,979.21	17.77%
	$2,924,760.42 97.89%	$7,475.66 0.25%	$9,948.31 0.33%	$8,536.15 0.29%	$5,527.21 0.18%	$31,606.41 1.06%	$2,987,854.16	

PATIENT AR

Delinquent receivables are the percentage of total accounts receivable that are more than thirty days past due. This metric should be broken into separate numbers for both the patient side and the insurance side, as depicted in the example of a single practice's accounts receivable "Patient AR" chart above. The chart depicts how we visualize total patient receivables with each "tier" representing the credit rating we assign patients, based on OrthoFi's proprietary algorithm. Those patients who opt out of a credit check are represented in the "no check" group on the lowest tier of the chart.

The patient AR aging chart, for example, indicates this practice would have 1.53 percent patient receivable delinquency (0.29 percent + 0.18 percent + 1.06 percent). As stated previously, an excellent collections process would be represented by a delinquency rate of less than 3 percent, and receivables fewer than thirty days delinquent are typically not considered in delinquency percentages.

Default receivables are defined as the percent of total net production that is uncollectable. Although that sounds simple enough to calculate, offices frequently err when figuring their default percent, and it can skew their decision-making. We consider any delinquencies past 180 days as "uncollectable" and in default status for calculation purposes, even though we still think you should continue to attempt collections for these moneys. Although these accounts are sometimes eventually collected, moneys owed longer than 180 days have a low likelihood of collection and belong in your "default" calculations. Speaking of calculations, many offices make the mistake of calculating default rate from their AR total instead of net production, but default rate (or its converse, the collections rate) is the total aggregate amount, or percentage, gained from what you produce, and it's not calculated from the receivables number. Default receivables can be stated as the equation below:

DEFAULT RATE = MONEYS DUE PAST 180 DAYS / NET PRODUCTION

Being familiar with all of these AR terms and having an understanding of how they impact your business's bottom line are vital if you're going to manage your practice's finances intelligently. As increased flexibility in payment terms becomes increasingly important to practice success, knowing how to manage your receivables becomes paramount to avoiding unnecessary delinquency and default risk.

Managing Receivables: Batch or Kanban?

Now that we've described the different types of receivables that require monitoring, we need to let you in on a very useful secret—you can choose from two very distinct ways to manage those receivables (or any repetitive task).

Batch task management involves postponing a specific task until a later time and then doing all similar tasks at the same time for the sake of efficiency. At my own practice, for example, my team often waits to scan forms into patients' files until there's a big pile of similar documents, then tasks a young team member to scan them all in at once. Batching makes sense for menial tasks or items/processes that aren't time sensitive and where there's no penalty, or decrease in overall practice performance, incurred by doing the task later. But staying on top of collections for a lot of people with different payment arrangements—at differing stages of repayment—isn't one of them.

Kanban task management is a system developed and popularized by Toyota but now being used for lean management and just-in-time management in many industries, including orthodontics. Instead of waiting to do a necessary task until it can be completed with another group of similar tasks (batch), the task is done immediately. Toyota learned this concept by studying the behavior of grocery stores and observing how they managed their inventory. Stores didn't wait, for example, until all the milk was gone from their shelves before restocking it all at once. They were constantly restocking and rotating the older stock to the front to ensure it was purchased while it was still good. Managing the "inventory" of an orthodontic practice (your past and present patients) requires a similar strategy.

What does this have to do with collections? Just as there are two task-management styles, there are two types of customers with delinquent ARs.

1. The deadbeat: The rare person who puts the absolute minimum required down, then tries to scam the system by getting as much free treatment as possible before getting booted for nonpayment. In our opinion, these people are simply part of your "cost of doing business," and their impact can be minimized but cannot be absolutely avoided. Take your lumps from these (rare) patients and move on. But whatever you do, *don't* base your financial policies on a few bad actors who try to beat the system.

2. Everyone else: A good person who has either overspent or fallen on hard times. These people *want* to pay you but simply can't pay all their current debts. Big data shows this second type of patient makes up the vast majority of delinquent accounts, and when they're offered the kind of extended financing plans we've been discussing, they will usually pay. The trouble is that many offices exacerbate the negative impact of this type of delinquency by batching their AR duties and not following up with these patients until it's too late. We believe that *a large portion of most office's delinquencies are self-inflicted* because of ineffective policies and procedures. This is especially true when AR duties are the sole responsibility of one person. If they get too busy to work the AR, take a vacation, or catch the flu (you get the idea), the receivables can accrue, and patients who could have previously paid are now in arrears for over what they can afford to pay off.

Oftentimes, the end result of inadequate AR training or systems is a doctor resorting to the tactic of waiting until a patient has paid in full to remove their braces. Their excuse is that "people won't pay me if I take the braces off." But opting to keep a child hostage in their braces until their parents pay is, in our estimation, a questionable practice. These orthodontists could have avoided delinquency in the first place by using systems that can accommodate more patient income levels, while increasing their profitability and growing their practice—all at the same time.

> **WE BELIEVE THAT A LARGE PORTION OF MOST OFFICE'S DELINQUENCIES ARE SELF-INFLICTED BECAUSE OF INEFFECTIVE POLICIES AND PROCEDURES.**

Collection Protocols

Unfortunately, the majority of orthodontic offices still batch their collection processes by making collection calls on the first and fifteenth of the month, as time permits. But that kind of batch approach to collections doesn't yield optimal results.

> The key to collection success is to touch every delinquent account proactively from day zero of delinquency and then repeat that contact consistently thereafter.

Delaying that first contact greatly increases the risk of an AR passing thirty days, ensuring collection will get exponentially more difficult and uncomfortable. Once a patient is over a month's payment in arrears, getting things back on track becomes progressively harder. We depict a far better collection approach in the following systems protocol chart. To allow the convenience customers want, every patient is able to choose their preferred date to withdraw payment, which means we need to follow up on payment activity every day. Managed this way (and potentially enhanced with AI-driven software), it's possible to have at least 98 percent of your AR balance stay current, or 98.5 percent within ten days.

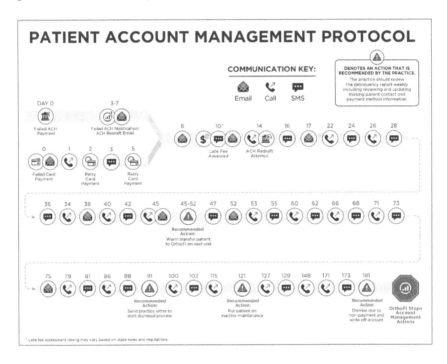

Turn On the Systems—Turn On Your Practice

If you're like most orthodontists, you prefer to focus on clinical treatment. But if you plan to grow your practice, your business systems will also need some love. Although everyone wants to grow, not everyone is ready to grow. The data we've amassed clearly shows being accessible, persistent, and flexible with patients will generate additional starts. But you need great systems in place if you're going to "seize the day" each and every day, maximizing your opportunities in a way that's sustainable.

One of the primary keys to collection success is to start with the end in mind—the same way you do when doing clinical planning. And it's how you should treat patients when it comes to their payments too. Respect is vital to everyone, and patients who owe you money are far more likely to work with you on that overdue balance if they feel like they're being "worked with" on the issue, rather than hounded. Although your end goal is the successful collection of payment, we recommend changing your approach (if you're not doing it already) by engaging with patients in a vigilant, consistent, and professional manner that always conveys respect. This systems chart shows you how to leverage that kind of flexibility.

But what do you do when a disruption (such as COVID-19) occurs, and normal business practices and expectations seem to evaporate? Such situations pose unique challenges to business owners, but your best defense is forecasting derived from large warehouses of data. If you're trying to rationalize operating costs and staffing changes with the least amount of disorder and hardship for your team, you'll need to be able to see what the numbers project about your practice's future income in order to plan ahead successfully. Knowing your projected collection rate, for example, can be helpful in planning costs, staffing hours, and headcount reductions during a period of industry disruption. These key numbers forecast current trends so that you can get ahead of the curve, no matter what direction it seems to be going.

What's Up Next?

In part III of this book, we're going to take a deep dive into the topic of how to best convert your prospects into patients who opt for same-day starts (SDS), since that's what the data shows the majority of orthodontic patients prefer. We'll examine the factors most likely to motivate those seeking your expertise to begin their recommended treatment right after their new patient exams. When patients don't choose an SDS, we'll teach you how to encourage them to start their treatment by improving your team's follow-up protocols. This section of the book will also show you how to implement the information in the previous chapters and turn everything we've already discussed into sales and business practices that will help you increase your patient starts right away.

Takeaways for Risk Management

- Many people will willingly pay you more total money for treatment if you allow them to make a lower down payment and a lower monthly payment as part of a longer repayment plan.
- Collections and receivables data prove using flexible financing can gain you millions in profitability while risking an overall default rate below 2 percent.
- OrthoFi data shows between 6 and 10 percent of people will pay interest for the affordability of an extended payment plan (possibly more in recessionary environments).
- Offering $500 down and $150 per month seems to be a key landmark for people seeking affordable plans.
- Instead of demanding big down payments or monthly payments, the smart way to manage risk is by charging interest to both disincentivize people from extending plans and hedging incremental default for those customers who need lower monthly payments.
- You can maintain best practice delinquency rates if you adopt a kanban management protocol that is courteous and consistent starting from day one.

Part III

CONVERSION DEEP DIVE

n this part of the book, you'll learn how to apply everything we've presented thus far to increase your practice's conversion rate by providing maximum patient benefit. Believe it or not, deciding you want to make more money and offering same-day starts as your mechanism to buy a bigger house is not the right approach. Offering difficult-to-achieve operational convenience and fabulous service will create more value in your office, and the patients—and profit—will follow. Money is a consequence of excellence and not a goal.

We'll show you how to use the concepts and strategies from previous chapters to offer improved patient value that will automatically raise your conversions in smart, quantifiable ways. Our objective is to equip you to put the information we've presented to practical use and turn everything we've already discussed into actionable business steps that are good for both your patients and your practice. After tackling the topic of how to best evaluate and measure your conversions, for example, we'll demonstrate how to improve them using pertinent patient data in the most practical and profitable way. You'll learn how to apply our proven methods to help your practice and every patient seeking your orthodontic expertise—since they're predicated on you getting better at offering and providing people with what they already want and need: quality orthodontics that are professional, friendly, affordable, and convenient.

We understand that no orthodontist wants to be perceived as a salesperson, and any perception of sales in our business as healthcare providers tends to be frowned upon. But in his book *To Sell is Human*, Daniel Pink correctly points out that we're all in sales—from car salesmen to cardiothoracic surgeons. In orthodontics, starting a patient in treatment happens as part of a sales process, and understanding how that sales process should work in your office is actually beneficial for your patients.

How so? Because we're confident you only recommend treatment when it's optimal for your patients, right? And we presume you're confident that your treatment is better than what they might get elsewhere, especially in a DTC shop, or many of the other options patients have for treatment, correct? On that good-faith basis, it's in everyone's best interest for the patient to follow your recommendation and start with you.

Accepting that you can implement a fundamentally sound sales process without sacrificing your integrity or being "salesy"—while actually helping your patients—is a key step in igniting the growth potential of your office. In the upcoming pages, we'll teach you how to use an interactive, automated, customer relationship management (CRM) solution to optimize your new patient onboarding experience so your practice is positioned for a steady stream of same-day conversions and revenue growth. Whether you choose to use OrthoFi in your practice or not, the fundamentals are the same and universally successful.

8

RATE YOUR SUCCESS WITH TREATMENT-RECOMMENDED CONVERSION

If you are not taking care of your customer, your competitor will.

—BOB HOOEY

Orthodontists with traditional practices are facing a growing army of competitors revolutionizing the industry and patient expectations. What's a self-respecting doctor to do? Play offense. That means outsmarting and outperforming your competitors with a two-pronged, winning strategy predicated on using better data and systems to provide the best quality orthodontic care. To do this well, you'll need to apply the data-proven business principles we're going to discuss in this chapter, then implement a tracking process that follows your patients along their new patient journey—measuring when they start and when they don't. It's that simple. But the protocol changes needed for success don't happen by themselves, and action is required to succeed using these two steps in our new industry environment. Sticking with the way you've always done things will make it progressively more difficult to win patients who are ready to start because patients love the convenience of getting started without having to make extra trips to your office. Convenience is a premium in today's society, and customers are demanding simplified approaches that are quicker and easier for them to access. If you can't provide those, they'll find someone else who can—even if it unwittingly sacrifices the clinical quality they receive.

> CONVENIENCE IS A PREMIUM IN TODAY'S SOCIETY, AND CUSTOMERS ARE DEMANDING SIMPLIFIED APPROACHES THAT ARE QUICKER AND EASIER FOR THEM TO ACCESS.

High-performance DTC companies with solid balance sheets are placing big bets on convenient orthodontic treatment, and they're racing to fill the vacuum created by their weaker competition: those practices unable or unwilling to respond to consumer trends. To quote a Chinese proverb, "When the winds of change blow, some people build walls, while others build windmills." This saying sums up what it looks like to play offense in the business world, where growth occurs as a result of making the most of every opportunity, and it's no different for the orthodontic industry. Smart and successful practices, for example, have used industry disruption to evaluate, then advantageously reconfigure their approach to patient-acquisition processes. By streamlining their new patient process to be effective for in-person or virtual consult environments, for example, many have emerged victorious with higher same-day starts and contracts and better overall conversion rates.

Innovate to Compete

For those practices unwilling to innovate, the statistics are grim. Even before recent industry disruptions, market data showed the average patient was seeing 2.5 orthodontists before deciding on treatment. Since its inception, we've used OrthoFi's software to amass and share data about how that impacts you, and it's not good. As soon as a patient leaves your practice, our data shows they're 20 to 50 percent less likely to start (depending on whether they've scheduled a return appointment). The growing popularity of virtual ortho consults is only intensifying that trend, which means you'll have to work even harder to connect with patients and convince them to choose you for their orthodontic treatment. To help you cope successfully, we'll delve more deeply into patient demand curves in chapter 9.

Emergent competition isn't the only factor making it harder for patients to choose your practice. So is decision fatigue. Decision fatigue is a form of mental stress psychologists say is a common reaction to the continuous decision-making required in everyday life. This cognitive response makes it easier to say "no" to small impulse buys, but harder to say "yes" to larger buys that will upset a person's financial status quo with another monthly payment. Similarly, choice overload can make people feel overwhelmed if they're offered too many treatment options or provided with too much detail about those options. If people have a hard time processing and assessing choices, they'll be less likely to choose anything at all. A lot of prospective patients may seek relief from the stress of decision fatigue and choice overload by simply walking away from the NPE without opting for any treatment at all. The point of streamlining every step of the presentation process during an NPE is to anticipate and remove such patient barriers—both physical and psychological—making it easier for patients to discern the value in your services and say yes to treatment.

The Importance of Your TRC Score

Just remember, consumers won't agree to start treatment if you don't provide the motivation (i.e., give them what they want). Your numbers will tell you how well you're doing with that, which is why it's more necessary than ever to intimately understand what's actually happening in your practice, rather than relying on what you think is happening. Measuring your rate of treatment-recommended conversions (TRC) acts as a critical scoreboard of your performance, and it's easily calculated using the equation:

TRC = #STARTS/#RECOMMENDS

Once you start tracking your TRC, you'll know how likely prospective patients are going to be to say "yes" when you recommend treatment. When asked at postmeeting cocktail parties, most orthodontists boast their golf scores are below 85, and their conversion percentage is above 85. Predictably, this estimate is typically overinflated. You may be surprised to find your TRC rate is also lower than you thought it would be.

This is why calculating your TRC "score" is essential to understanding the status of your business. Doing so enables you to discern which factors are increasing or decreasing your conversion rate and identify how to improve it. Some important factors influencing your current TRC will include the following:

- Ease of your scheduling system
- Number of appointments you require to put braces on
- Efficacy and timeliness of your new patient processes
- Affordability of your treatment plans
- Accuracy of your measured and analyzed performance using key performance indicators (KPIs)

The Difference between Sales and Marketing

When considering the process necessary to motivate customers to consume the essential products and services you provide, it's useful to clearly define the terms "marketing" and "sales"—two terms that are often misunderstood, misused, or unnecessarily feared in healthcare. Knowing the difference between marketing and sales, and using each of them strategically, is going to be key to your business success for the following reasons.

Marketing refers to the information you offer prospective customers about what services you provide and why they should care. Most people's favorite radio station is WIIFM—"What's In It For Me" radio. While it is important to establish yourself as a local authority (see the great book *Authority Marketing*, by Adam Witty and Rusty Shelton), a lot of orthodontists focus their messaging only around why they're great—where they went to school, what awards they've won, their status as Invisalign providers, or how cute their kids are—when people mostly only care about what value you bring them. They want to know about your products and

SUPERIOR BUSINESSES NOT ONLY PROVIDE PREMIUM PRODUCTS OR SERVICES, BUT THEY ALSO EXCEL AT COMMUNICATING THE VALUE PROSPECTIVE CUSTOMERS WILL GAIN BY CONSUMING OR UTILIZING THEM.

services and how easy or difficult it will be to utilize or consume what you offer. Superior businesses not only provide premium products or services, but they also excel at communicating the value prospective customers will gain by consuming or utilizing them.

Sales is the process of converting a prospective customer into an actual customer. That's it. Yet many in healthcare have a seemingly allergic reaction to the word and implicitly assume a negative, subjective connotation to anything that might involve "sales." Doctors tend to negatively conflate sales with having to compromise their integrity in a way that's disingenuous to the needs of the patient—as if the desire to make money is replacing all other factors in their recommendations. Since this does occasionally occur, albeit rarely, it's incumbent on doctors to restrict their treatment recommendations to those they would suggest for their own family members—something the vast majority of doctors already do. The integrity of your treatment recommendation is sacrosanct in the sales process we recommend.

With integrity-based diagnosis and treatment plans being your standard of care, it stands to reason the patient would be better served by initiating treatment and worse off by not following your treatment recommendation. Therefore, converting a prospective patient/customer to an actual customer is in that patient's best interest. Herein lies the foundation of integrity-based sales. In this context, the formulaic definition of treatment-recommended conversion we provided simply measures how successfully your marketing message communicates the value of your services to your prospects.

Although your TRC rate will tell you the effectiveness of your marketing and sales process, it won't tell you why your conversion rate is high or low. To know that, you'll have to individually assess each step of your patient intake process to identify what works and what doesn't. Gathering and analyzing such data enables you to distinguish the positive and negative factors in your patient intake process so you can improve it.

The Days You Work Matter

Have you ever wondered which day of the year is busiest for the majority of orthodontic practices? We did, too, so we collected and analyzed patient-visit numbers from 2014 to 2020 to find out. After evaluating our results, we were surprised to find that production was highest on Martin Luther King Day. In fact, MLK Day significantly outproduced all other days of the year, every single year, as you can see from the lines on the graph below that point to MLK days from 2014 through 2017. The graph depicts our starts-per-day since the inception of OrthoFi and shows how results have scaled over time as valuable data started pouring in. With the exception of the COVID-19 period, this chart looks similar as of the publishing of this book. This is a good example of how data can drive better processes, since knowing the busiest day for orthodontic practices will help ensure services are available when patients are seeking them most actively. The next time you plan to close the office and spend MLK Day skiing, remember this chart.

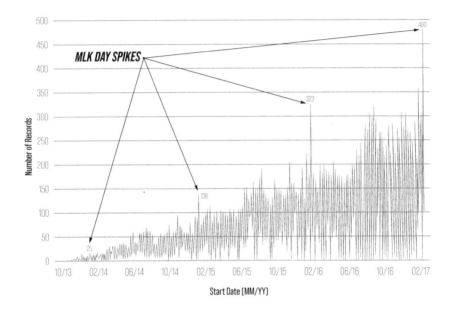

The likely reason for this phenomenon is that MLK Day is always on a Monday, and Mondays tend to be the busiest day of the week in the majority of offices anyway. It's also a national holiday, so schools are closed too. And because this holiday falls in January, right after insurance plans reset or initiate, and HSA and FSA accounts are freshly stocked, start rates are already primed to go up. Taking all these factors into account, it's obviously a great holiday to keep your office open and available to patients.

Doctors who want to use the day to vacation with their own children might be wise to choose an alternate vacation schedule. You can always take the kids on vacation the following week and save a bundle on hotels and airfare by traveling at a time of lesser demand. That choice would make a lot of sense, considering staying open on MLK Day is likely to generate hundreds of thousands of dollars in production over the course of your career. Knowing that reveals the value measuring data provides from just one finding. There are many others.

The Link between Fees and Conversions

If you're new to measuring TRC, you need to remember it's measured by the number of patients who actually start—as opposed to those patients to whom you simply recommended treatment and presented fees. Although TRC may seem to yield a lower number than what you're used to looking at, it's a much more accurate measure of how well your practice is really doing than the traditional "case acceptance" metric (#starts/#NPE). This metric can provide very misleading results if your number of new patient exams isn't constant or you have variability in your recall inflow/outflow rate.

Also of note: If you switch to using a software-based measurement of your TRC versus the traditional way of letting your treatment coordinator self-track it on a spreadsheet, expect the software calculation to yield a lower TRC rate. That's because many TCs don't accurately measure their own performance and inadvertently create an artificially inflated TRC. This kind of subjective assessment equates to the way golfers' self-reported scores don't usually reflect the handful of times they took casual liberty with the rules of the game. No golf tournament would allow this kind of subjective or lenient self-assessment to determine the outcome, and neither should you. This is why using data analytics is so crucial: it provides an objective way to gauge performance and results.

As we discussed in part II of this book, a major factor impacting your TRC is the affordability of the down and monthly payments you require. Unfortunately, a lot of orthodontists haven't caught on yet. Faced with the challenge of how to respond to increasing industry competition, for example, most orthodontists instinctively react by lowering their fees. Knowing that, we wondered how closely the total fee of treatment really related to TRC. Our important, and somewhat unexpected, findings are represented by the data in the chart below.

TX RECOMMENDED COVERSION VS AVG. TREATMENT FEE

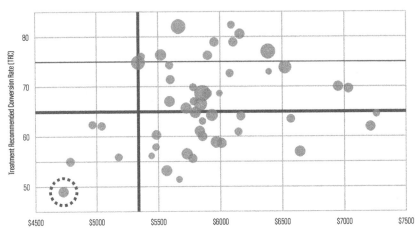

This bubble chart shows the correlation between fees and conversion rates, with the Y-axis indicating TRC (the percentage of patients who say yes to recommended treatment) and the X-axis, an average treatment fee. The bubbles represent practices from around the country with the size of the bubble an indicator of the size of the practice. Pricing theory would normally lead you to assume that the graph should have a general trend of upper left to lower right (higher price yields lower conversion), but that's not the case.

To analyze this further, X- and Y-axis lines were added to the graph, with the horizontal line representing the benchmark conversion percentage of 65 percent and the vertical line indicating a $5,400 treatment fee. Keep in mind that a TRC over 65 percent is considered good, and a TRC above 75 percent is deemed excellent. You may notice the bottom left-hand corner of the graph shows the lowest conversion rate, combined with the lowest TRC. This means that out of all OrthoFi practices assessed, the offices with the lowest average fee also had the lowest TRC—a finding that surprised us when we first saw these numbers! What this data makes clear is that building your growth strategy on enticing customers with low fees to win conversions is a misguided approach refuted by measured outcomes.

As counterintuitive as it may seem, there really isn't any correlation between price and conversion on fees ranging from $5,300, all the way up to $7,000 (and potentially higher). But a lot of orthodontists lose faith in the data, as we still see so many reacting to increased competition by lowering fees or doing a lot of discount promotions to win customers. Instead, you should be countering a slipping conversion percentage by looking at all factors other than treatment fee that may be contributing to your lower conversion rate—especially if you're a lower-priced provider whose fee is under $5,000 for full treatment.

FOCUSING YOUR MESSAGING AROUND AFFORDABILITY AND QUALITY, INSTEAD OF YOUR TOTAL PRICE FOR TREATMENT, WILL BE THE KEY TO INCREASING THE NUMBER OF YOUR CONVERSIONS.

Simply put, an excellent conversion rate is the product of much more than any one single factor, including overall cost.

Any good sommelier knows people automatically associate a wine's price with its quality. And an orthodontist can't practice in Detroit like I do without seeing that the automotive industry has put a lot of people with Buick budgets into Cadillacs. Even the high-end import brands have seen huge growth in their private and corporate leasing programs by making high-quality vehicles more accessible to consumers by offering lower monthly rates. Our data confirms that incredibly powerful business principle: people prefer higher quality to lower cost—as long as it's affordable.

It's no different for our industry. Focusing your messaging around affordability and quality, instead of your total price for treatment, will be the key to increasing the number of your conversions. In other words, your actual total fee for orthodontic treatment is less important than whether you make it affordable monthly—especially if you are charging less than $7,500. To nearly all consumers, price is related to quality, whether they're looking at a car, a home appliance, or healthcare. Within reason, people expect to pay a higher price for higher quality, and that's the way it should be. So don't be afraid to set your fees at the higher end, as befits the higher quality of the treatment you provide. At my own practice, I know my team is delivering outstanding value to each and every patient we see, and even though we're often charging a healthy fee, our extended financing often makes us the most affordable.

Online Forms Are Key

OK, so here's a question that may (or may not) keep you up at night: How do patient intake forms affect your conversion rate? In case you don't know or don't care, we have news for you. You definitely should care! The numbers we've amassed on this topic reveal a direct, interactive relationship between the timely completion of intake forms and same-day-contract rate—a rate we've already shown to have a massive correlation to your overall conversion rate. Wanting to know the specifics, we dug deeper to see the hidden picture the data was telling.

We looked at two cohort groups over a two-year period at the top and bottom ranges for same-day-contract rate—then paired them with their "urgent" insurance-eligibility check rate. When we looked at the median of both metrics for each cohort group, we were astonished to find such a clear correlation between the two factors, with the median same-day-contract rate of 63 percent for the top fifty practices, compared to a 10 percent same-day-contract rate for the bottom fifty practices. Although this data excludes practices with zero same-day-contracts because they require multistep consults before starting treatment, the connection between a low contract rate and urgent check rate to verify patient insurance was still crystal clear.

Looking at the data from a different angle, we see that the top-fifty group only had an immediate urgent insurance check rate of 16 percent (i.e., 16 percent of their eligibility verifications came in less than two hours before their exam, versus the bottom-fifty group, which had a higher urgent insurance check rate of 27 percent).

This gives you an excellent idea of why analyzing data is so fascinating: just looking at the numbers tells you one thing, but asking the data the appropriate questions can tell a different and more enlightening story. If you just look at the superficial numbers, you might surmise that the automated forms are working relatively well and consistently and that forms sent out automatically can achieve a very nice 70 percent fill rate, even in the lowest-performing offices—which is true. Simply automating the form delivery in a mobile-friendly format made a HUGE difference in how many people filled in the information before their appointment. However, if you dive a layer deeper, you'll find there is a 65 percentage point difference in the same-day-start rate between the two groups, which is absolutely monumental relative to the impact on your practice.

Now you might ask yourself why the same-day-contract rate is so much lower in that group when the urgent insurance check rate was only eleven points higher. The answer is simple and twofold:

1. The offices with the higher SDS rate were proactively reaching out and encouraging people to complete unfilled forms, while at the same time setting expectations for their exam, including the ability to start treatment the same day.
2. Treatment coordinators were able to present the total out-of-pocket cost in a timely fashion during the exam since insurance benefits had been verified ahead of time.

It's safe to assume those practices put more energy into making sure everything was set up to get the SDS before the patients arrived, using every procedure we recommend—from the initial, high-impact patient call to a thorough confirmation call protocol set for within forty-eight hours ahead of the exam. They were playing offense, meaning they weren't waiting around to see if the patient filled the forms out before the exam. Instead, they were proactively monitoring their form-fill rate, then proactively reaching out to those people who hadn't yet filled out their forms. This approach lessens the chance of the patient procrastinating until the night before the exam (or the morning of the exam) to fill out their online health and insurance forms. It also allows the treatment coordinator to set expectations for what will happen at the exam—including the option to start the same day if treatment is recommended.

If the first time the prospective patient or parent considers the potential of starting that day is after the fees have been presented, it is very difficult to encourage the convenience of starting without seeming pushy. Preexam consideration is the key to same-day starts.

We know this approach works because the data clearly shows practices with lower urgent check rates confirming insurance eligibility (secondary to unfilled forms before the exam) will see higher same-day-contract rates.

Once we saw what the numbers were telling us, the correlation seemed so logical and obvious. Insurance carrier hold times, or the unavailability of information, often prevent treatment coordinators from being able to verify a patient's coverage and make it impossible to present a full financial picture to a patient (or financially responsible party). We realized that having to conduct last-minute eligibility checks in the office to verify insurance coverage could easily make a patient less inclined to start treatment that day if the verification process hit a snag. Bypassing this issue by providing fully interactive online forms to patients before they come for a new patient exam, then verifying the insurance benefits in advance, is now a critical piece in enabling same-day starts. Patients of practices using software providing mobile-friendly online forms can complete all intake information from home, including insurance information, without having to print or email anything back to the practice. Not only is that most convenient for busy patients, but it also allows tracking of how, and when, these forms are completed.

If a patient with insurance hasn't completed their intake forms at least two hours prior to the exam, for example, we consider that an urgent eligibility check. But overall, we've found that more than 75 percent of our forms are completed before the exam date due to automating the process. We realize those rates can vary wildly across practices, due to inconsistent confirmation calls and the variability of office call scripting that's meant to inform patients about the importance of completing online forms prior to the exam. When those conversion factors are done right, however, it can make a huge difference in your TRC rate. Issues like this are what we refer to as patient "barriers," and eliminating them will raise your SDS conversions.

Now that we've explained how to measure and think about conversions, we need to show you how to prioritize the same-day starts that will fuel your practice growth. In a perfect world, every person who needed treatment would opt to start their treatment the same day. When executed properly, this is the best-case scenario for every doctor, but it's important to remember that's what orthodontic consumers want too. Time is everyone's most precious asset, which is why providing the convenience of same-day starts is definitely a win-win: it saves busy patients and parents valuable time.

Takeaways for Treatment-Recommended Conversion

- TRC is the most accurate metric to measure sales performance.
- Calculating your TRC is essential to understanding the status of your business.
- Identifying what factors are increasing or decreasing TRC is the first step to improving it.
- The average patient will see 2.5 orthodontists before deciding on treatment. As soon as a patient leaves your practice, the chances of them starting treatment with you drops 20 to 50 percent if they haven't scheduled a return appointment.
- Gathering patient and insurance information *before* the appointment via mobile-friendly online forms and then playing offense by proactively setting expectations utilizing a well-scripted confirmation call are of increasing importance to facilitate same-day starts.

9

INCREASE SAME-DAY STARTS TO GROW

Every minute you spend in planning saves 10 minutes in execution; this gives you a 1,000 percent return on energy!

—BRIAN TRACY

Same-day starts are arguably the single most important driver of a practice's growth and success. We've said that before, and we won't stop saying it until every doctor gets it: 100 percent of all patients who choose to get their braces put on the same day of the new patient exam also sign the treatment contract and start payment. Duh, you might think. That's so obvious! What may not be so obvious is that those SDS patients don't just fall out of the sky and into treatment. Understanding the financial principles illustrated previously and implementing a robust and repeatable sales process is essential to offering same-day service that doesn't come off as pushy or "salesy."

Many of you have spent a lot of time dialing in your clinical management systems to where they are virtually on autopilot, but a lot of you have neglected your marketing and operational systems.

> WE WON'T STOP SAYING IT UNTIL EVERY DOCTOR GETS IT: 100 PERCENT OF ALL PATIENTS WHO CHOOSE TO GET THEIR BRACES PUT ON THE SAME DAY OF THE NEW PATIENT EXAM ALSO SIGN THE TREATMENT CONTRACT AND START PAYMENT.

Systems touch everything, from the obvious areas of collections and scheduling to things as seemingly trivial as phone call management. Harnessing the power of great systems can optimize your team while better serving your customer's needs with processes that are consistent, repeatable, and sustainable. That means implementing logical, data-driven systems is going to be fundamental to the growth and well-being of your practice.

Unfortunately, some doctors have to learn that fact the hard way, and I was one of them! Until a few years ago, my team and I were tiptoeing around our prospective patients during new patient exams, trying not to be "pushy" with people. No doctor or treatment coordinator wants to feel like a high-pressure salesperson, and we certainly didn't either. But bending over backward in an effort to avoid marketing our skills to people who'd sought us out and come into our office to receive those very skills was pretty illogical! I had missed the fact that we weren't giving the patients what they actually wanted— which was to get their braces on quickly and conveniently. Now that technology has made everything faster, attention spans have grown shorter, and pretty much everyone wants things done immediately for the sake of convenience.

When I started thinking about how busy everyone's lives are, and what I would want if I was the one making the effort to come into the office with my children, I realized my team and I had been using the wrong approach. We'd been projecting our own misplaced assumptions onto people coming to get braces, knowing no one likes to be sold something they don't actually want. But those assumptions were false and illogical since patients had already chosen to expend their time and energy to seek out our services.

It finally dawned on me that giving people what they already wanted wasn't "salesy," but was actually adding value to their treatment experience. Presenting them with timely information and an efficient process that facilitated treatment quickly and effectively would actually benefit them the most. My eureka! Mom:ent provided the comprehension that everyone appreciates more efficient appointments and getting as much done as possible in the least amount of time. Not only that, formulating and offering the optimal choice to people during an NPE relieves them of the stress of having to configure a best-case orthodontic scenario with an array of information they don't really understand. That's where you come in. You're the expert, after all!

> *SALES IS NOT A DIRTY WORD. IT SIMPLY MEANS GIVING YOUR CUSTOMERS/PATIENTS THE VALUE THEY'RE SEEKING AND CONVERTING PROSPECTIVE CUSTOMERS INTO PATIENTS.*

Prospective patients coming into your office are obviously expecting you to provide the information they're consciously seeking, but it's incumbent on you to provide the added value of a proven, seamless, no-hassle process that preps them for starting their quality treatment the way the data shows they want it—quickly, conveniently, and affordably. The following concepts will enable you to do that in a way that jumpstarts your SDS conversions:

- *Sales* is not a dirty word. It simply means giving your customers/patients the value they're seeking and converting prospective customers into patients who start treatment at the time of the NPE.
- Real value for patients is created through strategic processes, sequence, and scripting.
- Gold-standard integrity means seeking to benefit your patients at all times.
- Being proactive and resolving objections or barriers before a patient encounters them is key to achieving more SDS conversions.
- Patients are customers who need value at every step of the process.
- The confirmation call, forms, and consultation should be carefully planned out, with the objective that everyone who comes for an exam knows it's possible to start treatment, if recommended, the same day.

We'll describe the effective SDS "onboarding" process we recommend in a Mom:ent. But first, let's reflect on the data that's impacting your practice daily. If a person does not get their braces on the day of their NPE—but does sign the treatment contract and makes a down payment—98.6 percent of them actually start. That's great to know, right? Especially for your aligner or digital indirect bonded cases. Although you might occasionally have someone decommit, almost everyone continues once they sign the contract and make a down payment. We speak with lots of doctors who are worried patients will default if they make a low down payment on an Invisalign case, but the reality is, this rarely happens. That one fact alone should allow you to confidently submit for aligner fabrication (without having fully covered your cost)—plus collect two monthly payments before the trays are actually delivered and the lab bill is due. Conversely, requiring all Invisalign patients, or any patient really, to make a high down payment before starting treatment is a growth killer that doesn't actually offer much protection from default.

The Numbers Don't Lie

Looking through the lens of data, there are several more growth and no-growth outcomes you need to see in order to understand why our process acts as such an effective playbook for each one. Remember, these scenarios aren't just our best-guess opinions but are reliable, predictable conclusions based on solid data.

CONVERSION RATES

100% — SAME-DAY STARTS

98.6% — SAME-DAY CONTRACTS

80.4% — SCHEDULED STARTS

49.4% — NON-SCHEDULED STARTS

- If a person neither gets their braces put on nor signs the contract on the day of their NPE—but they *do* schedule their start/records visit the same day as the NPE—the likelihood they will start is 80.4 percent. This isn't nearly as nice as 100 percent or 98.6 percent, but an 80 percent conversion rate is still positively stratospheric compared to that of most orthodontic offices. In the past, we never asked people if they'd like to schedule their start appointment when they were in the office. The patient typically stated they needed to "go home and think things over and call us with any questions" or to "talk things over with Dad," then we would "give them a call next week to answer any questions." Our response to that was to say, "OK." Now we know that simply asking people to get their return appointment on the books before they leave the office dramatically increases the likelihood that person will become a patient.

- What happens if a person leaves the office without braces, without signing the contract, and without scheduling their next appointment? *Chances of conversion decrease to 49.4 percent!* That means if the patient leaves the office without starting or scheduling, the likelihood of you treating them is about the same as a coin flip and decreases even more when your pending management procedures aren't buttoned up.

- If you have a practice still using multistep consultations (not a good idea), your conversion percentage should be measured one time for *all* exams during which you recommend treatment and not for all those who come back for a two, or three-step, consultation. If you have a three-step consult and say, "My conversion is 90 percent," your true conversion is surely not reflected by that high percentage. Many people won't come back for the extra consults and start treatment, so the number of consults ends up artificially inflating the true conversion rate and giving you a data set that misleads you into believing you're doing much better at conversions than you actually are. For example, if a patient comes to your office for an exam and you schedule another consult as your next step, but the patient gets a second opinion at another office and starts there the same day, measuring your conversion by when you recommend treatment (which you haven't done yet) won't capture the fact you lost that patient to a second opinion. For multistep consultations, case acceptance is a sounder measurement for sales performance, as it captures the total number of exams, but it's still an imprecise method. Besides, the multistep consult approach is a poor business practice that needs to be phased out as soon as possible.

Don't Fudge Your Conversion Numbers

Measuring your conversion rate incorrectly can certainly boost your ego, but it can also cause massive amounts of production to slip away from your practice. If you're measuring conversion percentage by the simple case acceptance metric (#starts/#new consults), you're doing it the old-fashioned way, and your conversion rate is not as precise as you think it is. Not measuring conversion at all is even worse. Are you wondering how I know that? Yup, you guessed right. I didn't bother measuring my conversion rate at my own practice for years, thinking I was doing pretty great in the TC room—until the data generated by clean conversion metrics revealed the harsh reality that my practice's conversion rate really stank! Our forty-five-day TRC (tracking if a patient converted within forty-five days of the treatment recommend) was 35 percent. Yikes!

CONVERSION SUMMARY CASE ACCEPTANCE WITH PHASE 2: 31.88%			
	45-DAY TRC FROM 8/17/2014 THROUGH 9/30/2014		
EXAM TYPE	**Tx RECOMMENDED**	**STARTS**	**TRC**
NEW PATIENT	110	33	30.0%
RECALL	26	14	53.85%
PHASE 2	10	5	50.0%
OBSERVATION	2	1	50.0%
TOTAL	148	53	35.81%

TRC for Spillane & Reynolds Orthodontics
when we first started OrthoFi, September 2014

And my office wasn't the only one. When we started looking at a lot of other practices, we discovered a disturbing trend: the performance of most doctors, when measured accurately, had conversion rates of 50 percent. But many of those doctors thought their conversions were closer to 80 percent. It's sobering to think about the huge amount of time, energy, and profit being wasted if you're only converting half of the patients to whom you recommend treatment—plus, not starting treatment isn't good for your patients either! So it's in their best interest (and yours) to increase your conversions, and the smartest place to start is by getting an accurate assessment of your real TRC. To do that, you'll need to use the correct calculation: the number (#) of patients who start treatment divided by the number (#) of patients who were recommended treatment (i.e., conversion % = #starts/#recommends). Once you know your current TRC, you can use it as a baseline against which to measure your future success as you implement the process we recommend to maximize the number of SDS conversions in your office.

A bare-bones version of that process can be summarized in the following six steps that will make a world of difference in your conversion rate, your profitability, and perhaps your continued ability to sustain your practice:

- The obvious first step to increasing the profitability of your practice is using effective marketing (as we've already detailed) to prompt more people to contact your office requesting NPE appointments. Once they do, when and how you answer the phones will impact the number of prospects that convert to SDS after their NPE.

- Priming people to start treatment the day of their NPE takes intentional planning and focusing on the key procedural steps facilitating same-day starts. We'll explain how to do that in a Mom:ent.

- If you can't put the braces on that day (or scan for aligners or digital braces), request that people sign the contract and start the down payment. You will be surprised how many say "yes" if you simply ask, and when they do, the data shows 98.6 percent of them continue to treatment. In Robert Cialdini's book *Influence,* he discusses the power of "commitment" as a principle of influence, explaining that people are much more likely to follow through with something once they commit to it.

- When people don't start treatment on the day of their NPE, be sure to communicate the convenience and benefit of scheduling their records/start. If they don't agree, your chance of converting the person into a patient drops below 50 percent the Mom:ent they walk out the door.

- If they don't start or schedule, be sure to have a defined and consistent pending follow-up process so that if people need more time to consider treatment, you are top of mind and available when they are ready to schedule.

- Measure and monitor your practice's TRC rate the correct way using the equation of Conversion% = #Starts/#Recommends.

New Patient Calls: The Data!

Learning how to optimize your team's phone interactions with prospective patients calling your office to make an appointment is the first step in attracting more new patients to visit your office for an NPE. It's essential you verify that incoming calls are being handled correctly and that people who call and schedule appointments are actually keeping them. Once they do, your highest priority is to make sure those people become patients. That may seem ridiculously obvious, but believe it or not, these basics are too often overlooked. Spending on marketing before you've implemented good phone and conversion procedures is like pumping air into a leaky tire. It may act as a temporary fix, but it's not a sustainable one. Instead of relying on stopgap measures, it's smart to establish a phone protocol that ensures inquiry calls turn into consults. The best protocol will address three crucial aspects of your team's phone interactions:

- *When* and *if* team members answer the phone is important because phone traffic picks up a lot during specific times of day and on particular days of the week. Most phone systems allow software that tracks "call handling," which will tell you the percentage of your answered calls on any given day, and the exact time they were answered as well. That's important to know, but the majority of doctors have no idea what percentage of their incoming office calls are being answered and how many are being missed. They only know that the people answering the phone seem busy. Knowing and improving your answered-call percentage—the goal here is 90 percent or better answered calls—is the single biggest key to unlocking practice growth. Obsessing about your latest Instagram post, TikTok office video, or how much you will spend on Google paid search does no good if the result of your marketing makes the phone ring and you don't answer. *In fact, you shouldn't even consider paid search if you don't know what your call handling rate is or if it is below 80 percent.*

- *How* teams answer the phone is vital to securing a scheduled appointment.
- *How fast* your team can schedule new patients is also a critical component of planning, as lengthening the booking window dramatically decreases the likelihood someone will do business with you.

When You Answer the Phone Matters

The time of day your team answers the phone is an overlooked aspect of office management in our industry, but one that can create some quick wins. Let's look at some data. The graph below displays the time of day a new patient exam is created. As you can see, after a small spike at 8:00 a.m., reflecting the team catching up on messages, there's a steady climb throughout the day until 1:00 p.m. in the middle of lunch, then a dip to 2:00 p.m., and then a bigger decline after 3:00 p.m. The afternoon decline could be the result of the afternoon rush of incoming patients, causing an overflow of calls not being answered or parents being preoccupied with after-school activities. Whatever the cause, the graph shows that calls drop off steeply at that time.

Number of NPEs Created by Time of Day

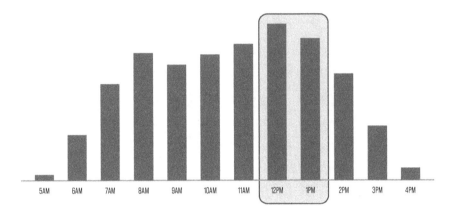

In case you missed it, the takeaway message should be shouting at you—that 26.5 percent of all exams are created between noon and 2:00 p.m. on the days that practices are open. Yet many new offices we onboard aren't answering their phones during lunch at all, choosing to use various types of voice mail or answering services instead. The typical reason they cite is "That's the way we've always done it," or "I can't get my team to staff the phones at lunch." You may think that callers will hear the recorded message and call back after lunch, which is possible. But they're also likely to keep calling other orthodontic offices until they get one with a live person answering the phone. If

26.5 PERCENT OF ALL EXAMS ARE CREATED BETWEEN NOON AND 2:00 P.M.

you're looking for a way to grow your practice, and you don't already answer your phones at lunch, doing so will be an easy, cost-effective way to spur growth. In fact, the data also suggests you should start answering the phones at 7:00 a.m. Monday through Friday because that's the time working families will call before they go to work.

In addition, the numbers show a higher percentage of exams are created on certain days of the week. Most patients call on Mondays, for example, with a decreasing number of calls occurring every day thereafter. Knowing that, you might be surprised to know we found that 9.7 percent of all appointments are scheduled on Fridays. So on a blended basis, approximately 29 percent of new patient exams (it's 34 percent in my office) were scheduled during workday lunch hours or on Fridays. That obviously means you need to have someone answering your phones at those times, even if you're not doing exams then. Nowadays, that doesn't require your scheduling team to come into the office because you can add cloud or remote access to your software and leverage call-forwarding technology to easily extend your hours. Doing so will yield results that easily cover any extra overhead expense.

As we mentioned previously, your goal should be to answer at least 90 percent of the calls that come into your office. Once you accomplish (and maintain) that goal, you can turn your attention to marketing activities which will make the phone ring even more. Wondering why you aren't growing? Look first at when you answer your phones and then consider the extra profitability provided by improving your customer service in this key area.

How You Answer the Phone Is Key

Unless you record and score each new patient call, tracking the quality of your phone team is a difficult thing to measure. But tracking your kept exam percentage (KeptNPE%) is easily calculated with the equation:

KEPTNPE% = KEPT EXAMS / SCHEDULED EXAMS

It's a practical, albeit indirect, performance indicator that gives insight into the customer service you're providing on new patient calls. Keeping KeptNPE% above 90 percent is a good goal to strive for, showing your phone team is efficient and friendly—two factors that facilitate high-quality customer interactions. When a person calls and gets a very warm feeling about your office, they'll be more likely to keep their exam. Conversely, a person turned off by your phone team is less likely to show up for their scheduled appointment.

Again, we have used Brian Wright and New Patient Group's phone training at my own practice with great results and recommend considering them as a first step toward improving your phone performance. (I have no relationship to this company other than gratitude for the results we've seen.) Historically, it's been understood that the key to successful phone interactions is ensuring your team has high energy and keeps calls short and sweet—while still providing a positive preview of what prospective patients can expect during their next visit. However, the real priority for optimal phone performance is training your team to recognize buying signals from prospective patients and using a dual-option close to take control of the phone call when scheduling a new patient exam. Incentivizing your team to learn and execute these phone skills will turbocharge your new patient flow.

How Scheduling Impacts Kept Exams

If your practice is running with a significant wait list (over two weeks) for prime-time exam appointments, you might be wondering at what point the wait will increase the odds of patients not keeping their exam. It's wise to think that way, and we wondered about that too, which is why we looked at the data to find out.

On the following "Kept Exam Decay" graph, the Y-axis is the kept exam percentage of those people that scheduled and kept an exam—while the X-axis displays the number of days from the date the exam was booked. The dashed line is for adults, the solid line is the average, and the dotted line is for kids. This graph depicts the gradual kept-appointment decline that occurred over time—a decline that grew steeper depending on how many days people had to wait to come in for their exam after it was scheduled.

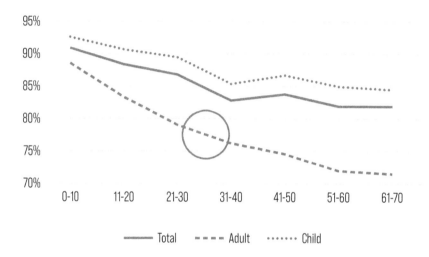

KEPT EXAM DECAY
(Days Between Date Scheduled and NPE Date)

——— Total - - - - Adult ······· Child

Unfortunately, almost 10 percent of prospective patients overall don't show up for the exams they book, with adults having a 13 percent no-show rate—even if they book for later the same day. To address that problem, we've learned the best strategy is one used successfully by other growth-oriented business models: overbook your TC's prime-time appointments for early morning and late afternoon slots, then hire a records tech to help with x-rays and pictures when, and if, the TC gets overwhelmed. Records techs are easy positions to fill and train, so this is a great growth-promoting strategy you'll want to implement right away. So when you're booking your exams, you may want to think like an airline and overbook a little to anticipate a 10 percent (or greater) no-show rate—especially during prime-time hours. See the previous section on booking windows for additional commentary.

In addition to the overall no-show rate depicted in the previous graph, you can see there's a steady decline in the kept exam rate after the first day. Adults fade faster than kids, and after three weeks there is over a 20 percent chance adults will not keep their scheduled exams. Because adult demand for treatment is usually less need driven and more spontaneous and want driven than treatment recommended for children, it's wise to schedule adult exams expeditiously when they're most motivated to start.

Declines in the rate of children's exams, on the other hand, tend to stay reasonably flat with only a percent or so drop over the first three weeks. That's likely because parents understand their children will need braces, so they plan and save accordingly. The decision to schedule and keep exams for children is much less spontaneous. But after three weeks, even the percentage of kept child exams drops off steeply.

The moral here is that if you're going to treat more adults, you'll want to intentionally plan to keep time open for them and schedule their NPEs as quickly as possible.

But for patients of all ages, you shouldn't have a wait list longer than three weeks.

Anything over that and the data suggests you're going to be losing a significant number of new patients. Once I realized the implication of these statistics for my own practice, I knew my team and I would need to reduce our exam time from sixty minutes (a common industry standard) to forty-five minutes to accommodate additional exams. That's not to say I opted to give our patients less doctor time. It meant strategically streamlining our patient onboarding process by acquiring as much information as possible before the patient arrived at the office and by making sure their insurance was already verified and their benefits were understood.

This approach is yet another great example of how being proactive and playing offense will be good for both your patients and your practice: collecting patient information ahead of time saves time during exams and frees up extra exam slots, allowing you to reduce wait times for new patient appointments. Shrinking your sixty-minute exams by fifteen minutes, for example, typically allows a minimum of one extra exam per day, with many doctors being able to accommodate two extra exams.

With mobile-friendly online forms and a good process like the one we've described, it's possible to have over 85 percent of your examined patients provide you with their health-history and insurance information (if applicable) before they arrive for the exam. This approach not only avoids wasted time waiting for forms and insurance checks but creates time for one or more extra exams per day. Perhaps most importantly, it primes new patients for same-day starts. If you could thin your wait list and fill that extra exam space four days per week—even a conservative forty weeks a year—and convert just half of those patients, you would generate eighty extra starts per year. At an average fee of $5,000 per start, eighty extra starts total $400,000 of additional production! Call me crazy, but we think paying yourself several hundred thousand dollars (per year!) to shorten your exams and streamline your patient intake process sounds pretty worthwhile. If you still have a heavy wait list after making those two changes, you should consider increasing your capacity with another TC or doctor in the practice, depending on your goals for growth.

Virtual Consults for Digital Success

Virtual consultations continue to increase in popularity as a way to stay connected with patients, so it's essential you consider how your patient onboarding processes will sync up to ensure your digital interactions are successful. Knowing how to navigate through these consults will ensure you're ready to deliver a best-in-class patient experience that naturally increases your conversions.

During the COVID-19 pandemic, virtual consults proved to be a practical, powerful way to check in with existing patients while onboarding new patients who couldn't come to your office physically. That's still true today, and they're also invaluable when your practice is flooded with more appointments than you can normally handle. Contacting patients by means of a virtual interface increases your team's efficiency, and at the same time, the convenience of these consults removes patient barriers to start. And as online consults grow in popularity, many practices are turning to cloud-based CRM software (of which OrthoFi is one example) to streamline their digital patient-acquisition workflow. Using such software to simplify your patients' virtual onboarding experience can really set your practice up for success. It's a very user-friendly process that has made doing virtual consultations much easier. Here is how the process works in our office using OrthoFi software:

- Days before the virtual exam, a series of texts and emails are sent to the family, asking them to fill out their insurance verification and health-history form online (this takes about six minutes).
- Back at the practice, the OrthoFi dashboard displays whether a patient's insurance has been verified and whether they've completed their health-history form. Those online forms will include questions about the kind and timing of treatment

the patient wants (and even asks about their hobbies) because your TC can use these insights to boost starts. If patients are slow responding, clicking a button sends them another automated or manual reminder text and email.

- The TC makes a preexam confirmation call to introduce the patient to the office and sets expectations for the virtual examination the next day. If the patient's online forms still aren't filled out, the TC emphasizes the importance of completing the forms and providing the requested information—especially any relevant insurance information.

- During the NPE, OrthoFi's patient-acquisition flow enhances the virtual consult by allowing the TC to send a working version of the payment slider for the patient to use remotely. Any of a number of streaming video applications (Zoom, FaceTime, Ring Central, Teams, Smile Snap, eTC:) can be used for the video communication aspect of the exam process.

- After a patient chooses their financing option, the software permits "sign at home" convenience so a patient can sign the contract and make their payment from home, without anyone from the office present. The patient is then scheduled for an in-person visit to begin their treatment.

Virtual consults can be just as effective as those conducted on-site when it comes to conversion rates. But when a conversion doesn't happen, it's essential to have a process in place that encourages patients to commit to scheduling a return appointment to start treatment. We'll dive deeper into the best ways to convert pending patients in the next chapter. Remember, if NPE patients leave your office without any commitment to return, your practice's conversion rate drops to under 50 percent. It's reasonable to infer the same decrease occurs if the virtual consultation ends without a contract being signed or an appointment scheduled.

Another strategy to mitigate no-show rates and facilitate better prime-time appointment productivity is to consider scheduling your retreatment exams as virtual consultations. As patients already treated in your practice, retreatment candidates are already familiar with your doctors, team, and systems, so they don't need (or want) the pomp and circumstance of a formal exam process. That factor alone makes virtual consultations the perfect solution for retreatment exams, particularly since they can be scheduled during the prime-time exam spots these patients seem to prefer, leaving those coveted in-office time slots open for NPEs. Since retreatment usually incurs a very low fee (retainers only) or dramatically reduced charges that barely allow a doctor to break even financially, they're the perfect patients to screen virtually. In our office, we have one set fee for retreatment (it differs slightly with braces versus aligners), which makes the financial conversation easy. Once signed up for retreatment, they can be scheduled in the clinic, rather than the exam room, freeing up valuable TC and exam room time.

Takeaways for Same-Day Starts

- Managing your team's phone skills is absolutely essential to the success of your practice. One easy step to growth is making sure your phones are answered starting at 7:00 a.m., during lunchtime, and on Fridays.

- Measuring your kept exam percentage (KeptNPE%) is an easy metric to grade the quality of service your phone team is providing.

- Remember that most people who call you want to get in to see you quickly. Be sure to provide them with rapid access to exams to keep your practice pipeline full.

- To increase the number of kept exams, slightly overbook your scheduled exams, especially with adults, and decrease exam time from sixty minutes to forty-five minutes. During high-demand times, add another records tech or cross-train a team member to handle TC overflow.

- Consider implementing the convenience of virtual exams in your practice to add value for both prospective patients and those wanting retreatment.

10

PENDING PATIENTS—
THE LEAKY BUCKET

It is not the most intellectual of the species that survives;
it is not the strongest that survives; but the species that
survives is the one that is able best to adapt and adjust
to the changing environment in which it finds itself.

—LEON MEGGINSON

Your prospective patients/customers are like drops of water flowing
into a bucket (i.e., your practice), and after they start treatment, they
gradually fill that bucket up. As you might surmise, having a full
bucket represents a practice working to full capacity and profitability,
which is terrific (and unusual) when it happens. Even better is when
a practice's bucket overflows because that means your business has

grown enough to warrant adding more capacity with another team member, doctor, or location. But just the opposite occurs if your practice bucket leaks because you're losing pending patients/customers due to deficiencies in your team, process, or technology.

Although you may think a leaky bucket has very little to do with an orthodontic practice, it's an apt analogy for offices that aren't doing well converting pending patients—losing the significant profitability they represent in the process. Many practices don't know their conversion rate or may calculate it incorrectly, so they don't have any optics to see how badly they're "leaking" patients, why it's happening, and how to fix it. That's true for you too. Without multiple data points to objectively measure the success of multistep patient interactions and the effectiveness of your office functions, it's impossible to diagnose the true status of your business.

Relying on your gut feelings to alert you when pending-patient loss is lowering your conversion rates is a suboptimal approach. Like any good doctor, you know it's necessary to diagnose the cause of underlying malaise in order to remedy it, and that's true for your practice too. A lot of us simply don't know how.

What's Your Pending Patient Plan?

When a person does not start treatment or sign a contract the day of their NPE, it's not the time to wing it. You need to have a well-scripted plan in place that always follows the same proven protocol. Doing so enables you to harness the power of an effective follow-up management process that ensures every pending patient will get the same ideal experience. If you opt for this approach, your team can respond like a well-oiled machine without skipping a beat. You can step back and let your TC take control of the conversation and guide a pending patient's next steps. To understand how advantageous that is for your practice, let's contrast a typical approach versus our recommended approach, assuming normal steps have failed to elicit a same-day start or to schedule a start.

The typical approach allows the responsible party to take charge of the conversation in a way that's almost always less productive. It usually sounds something like this:

TC: The doctor is recommending treatment.

Mom: I need to talk to Dad before I make any decisions.

TC: OK, go ahead and talk to Dad, and call me with any questions.

The patient proceeds to leave the office without any definitive decisions being made, and no scheduled start appointment or any expectation for a follow-up call is set.

The recommended approach begins like the typical approach, but the TC takes control of the conversation and establishes themselves as a busy person who is devoting time to help answer any questions:

TC: The doctor is recommending treatment.

Mom: I need to talk to Dad before I make any decisions.

TC: I totally understand. This is a very important decision. I'd like to set a time to follow up with you and answer any last questions you may have. I can make myself available to you on Tuesday or Wednesday. Which would you prefer?

Note how the TC takes control of the conversation and initiates a closing technique called the dual-alternative close. They will continue to use this technique by offering two choices to pick from until the appointment is scheduled.

Mom: OK, great. I can make Wednesday work.

TC: Fantastic. Do you prefer morning or afternoon?

Mom: Morning.

TC: Would you prefer ten or ten thirty?

Mom: Ten thirty would be great, thanks.

TC: Perfect. Please add that to your calendar, and I will give your cell phone a call to discuss questions and next steps.

This technique imbues your TC with an aura of professional authority that makes pending patients feel respected and valued. This is why asking a series of friendly questions in person, during the NPE, is the best way to set the expectation of a follow-up call. Although facilitating either an SDS or scheduled start before the patient leaves is always best, sometimes the parent isn't interested and any further attempts could seem pushy, alienating the patient/parent. In that case, keep in mind that calling them later may seem pushy as well.

Have you ever wondered how big businesses manage their follow-ups? They do it with customer relationship management systems like Salesforce® and with automated drip marketing. Such systems allow you to set the standard follow-up cadence you want to adopt, prompt you when it's time for a customer touch, and even send automated drip messages at designated times. Instead of having to remember to pull that pending report and make calls when you happen to think about it or have time (losing opportunities each day in between), the system pushes reminders to you when it's time for that particular contact opportunity. There is, of course, a fine line between excellent follow-up and being pushy, so be careful not to cross that line. And remember, the sequence stops if the patient starts treatment or doesn't want any more follow-up.

Patient Follow-Up That Works

If a patient doesn't sign the same day of their NPE and they don't schedule their start while in the office, the TC offers to "make themselves available" as described above. When a call doesn't get scheduled, our office initiates the following seven-step follow-up sequence:

- ✓ Twenty-four hours: Follow-up call. If leaving a message, be sure to set expectations by saying, "If I don't hear back from you, I'll follow up in a couple of days." This will make your next touch point seem more expected and less pushy.
- ✓ Three days (seventy-two hours): Text message.
- ✓ One week: First email (see email script below) + phone call.

"Thank you so much for taking time to visit with me and Dr. (Doctor's name) to review the benefits of orthodontic care. We look forward to having you as part of our practice and to designing (Patient's name)'s amazing smile! Call us today to get started.

Click here to download a free report that can help you understand key factors to consider when choosing an orthodontist: www.OrthoQuestions.com.

Thank you!"

- ✓ Two weeks: Text message
- ✓ Four weeks: Second email (see email script below)

"I'm not sure if you received my email from last week, but I wanted to follow up with you to see if you're ready to get started with (Patient's name)'s treatment or if you had any remaining questions. We look forward to welcoming you to the practice and providing the very best care. A beautiful healthy smile is not only important for (Patient's name)'s long-term dental health but can be life-changing in terms of confidence and future career success.

Click here to see how (Practice name) patients feel about their new smile.

[VIDEO] https://vimeo.com/151309125

Thank you!"

- Six weeks: Text message (with promo tease)
- Eight weeks: "Last chance" email (with limited-time whitening or similar promo)

In 2021, my practice started using OrthoFi's automated follow-up system that automatically prompts the TC when it's time for a patient/parent's follow-up call. It sends follow-up emails and texts with pre-determined scripting and sequencing as well. Although no TC wants to feel they're being pushy, being professional means being consistent. Most patients are very busy, and getting back to you is obviously not their number-one priority, so providing professional and friendly follow-up will impress your patients/parents if done properly. It will also increase the number of people who choose your office for their orthodontic needs.

What's a CRM?

Ask anyone in a "real" business if they use a CRM, and they'll answer, "Of course we use one. Are you crazy?" But ask any orthodontist what

CRM they use, and they will usually reply, "What's a CRM?" So you patiently explain it's an acronym referring to customer relationship management software like Salesforce, which helps companies interact with prospects in a consistent way that yields results. CRMs don't wait for someone to pull the reports; they push reminders and communication notes to teams daily and display when tasks are completed.

As an example, let's say you're an elite-level office set up for SDS (instead of multistep consults before starts), and 50 percent of your starts happen the same day as your patients' NPEs. On average, there's a fifty-fifty chance your remaining patients will start treatment at a later time, with half of those pending patients converting within the first two weeks. This pending period is such a critical time for facilitating conversions; waiting a week or longer between follow-up contacts with patients is self-inflicting poor outcomes when that's completely avoidable. By utilizing CRM software, you'll be able to track and manage pending patients as part of your new patient acquisition process—and do it in a way that optimizes their conversion rate most effectively.

THE DATA IS CRYSTAL CLEAR: THE MORE SDS, THE HIGHER YOUR CONVERSION RATE.

Pending Management: Seize the Day—Every Day

Retrieving pending patients and helping them choose treatment by showing them how they'll benefit is a high priority, but same-day starts/contracts will always be the optimal growth promoter for your practice. Period. We know that because data shows a linear correlation between the percentage of your starts occurring the same day you recommend treatment and your TRC. The data is crystal clear: the more SDS, the higher your conversion rate.

Even if your exam process is conducted perfectly, however, not everyone will start their treatment or sign a contract on the day of their NPE. Many people really do need to go home and talk to Dad, think about it, or get dental work done first. When that happens, your team needs to be ready to follow up with sequential, scripted phone and email contacts on a predetermined schedule over the course of the next eight weeks—with the first call being made just twenty-four hours after their treatment recommendation. This contact protocol is time well spent, because once a person leaves your office and becomes a pending patient, your proposed treatment is going to be competing with all manner of other distractions and expenses, as well as potential advertising from your competition. These factors will dramatically diminish the likelihood of that person starting the treatment they need in your office. Not convinced? The graph below displays that irrefutable data, showing a downward trend you can't miss.

DEMAND CURVE BY DAYS PAST NPE

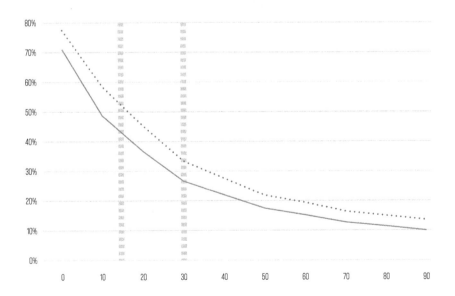

After a new patient exam, the graph shows the TRC on the Y-axis and what happens to patient conversions after time passes on the X-axis. The solid line represents adults, and the dotted line denotes kids, and the steep decline depicted for both shows why same-day starts/contracts are so important. As soon as a prospective patient walks out the door, the chances of them starting their recommended treatment fall off a proverbial cliff! In fact, this data shows the likelihood of your pending patients starting their needed treatment drops 20 percent the Mom:ent they leave, and decays further to 35 percent for children and 45 percent for adults, over the course of the next two weeks. Those sobering statistics may dismay the many offices that still do their pending patient follow-ups in batches every other week. If that's what your team does, you're probably reducing your chances of treating your pending patients by almost half—and not because of your treatment plan, clinical skill, or affordability—but because of your inadequate process.

Follow-Up Management Works!

So how effective is it to manage the follow-up process for pending patients? The chart below represents the difference between office teams who used the pending management tool in the OrthoFi software versus the teams who didn't. Although each office with the software had the ability to use the included pending management tool, some chose not to utilize that feature, enabling us to measure the obvious performance difference between those who used it and those that didn't.

	45-DAY TRC	90-DAY TRC
INACTIVE [Not Using Follow-Up Tool]	38%	44%
ACTIVE [Using Follow-Up Tool]	42%	52%
		Excludes Same-Day Starts

When we asked teams why they didn't choose to use the tool, they told us they thought patients would consider the follow-ups pushy, and that following up with patients wouldn't help encourage them to get the treatment they needed. We were surprised to find out they thought skipping follow-up calls and emails altogether wouldn't make any difference in patients' treatment decisions.

These false notions simply aren't true, and they conflict with accepted and well-understood consumer behavior norms. Although marketing principles pertaining to customer follow-up do indicate there's a point of diminishing return, that point is typically well beyond what the majority of practices act upon, and more significantly, well beyond their comfort zone. As in most other industries, there is meaningful value in pushing past that discomfort. Diligent follow-ups keep you and your pending patients interacting and engaged, reducing the chance that those patients will decide against starting their recommended treatment—or end up at another practice altogether. Those two extremes are exactly what the pending management software tool is designed to avoid. And that's why it works so well.

This reminder software simply keeps the TC adhering to a "best practice" follow-up sequence that's proven effective at galvanizing patients to start their needed treatment. Although the software makes remembering and organizing follow-up activities easier, you can certainly do it on your own, providing you stick to the fundamental schedule and scripting we outlined previously.

Here's how the tool works: using an interactive dashboard, the tool prompts you to complete the correct sequence of actions most likely to spur patients to start their treatment. Initially, the system automatically reminds your TC to populate the dashboard with a follow-up date and cite the reason any consult doesn't result in a patient starting treatment. After that, the dashboard displays all needed follow-up actions, along with pop-up reminders. The team updates these as they complete the suggested actions or make recall appointments during the eight weeks pending patients are managed by the system.

As the chart above indicates, this protocol works, improving the percentage of patients who opt to start their recommended treatment. In a four-hundred-start-per-year practice, for example, using the pending tool equates to twenty-eight additional starts and $160,000 in additional annual start revenue (assuming a $5,000 average case fee). Not bad for simply being persistent and consistent when following a pending-patient-management process. Doing so without a CRM will take up a lot of extra time that could be better spent facilitating more same-day starts or contracts.

The Moral of Our Business Story

Nearly all of the business knowledge we've shared in this book was not learned or acquired easily. It represents hard-won insight, wrested from our desperate response to the Great Recession and from big data gleaned from orthodontic consumer buying behavior. Back in 2007, we were leaking patients faster than we were converting them in our Metro Detroit offices, and we had no choice but to figure out why or go under. In survival mode, almost everything we had learned about financing and orthodontic collections got thrown out the window to fix those leaks. We desperately tried and tested several different strategies, including no down payments, low monthly payments, and high paid-in-full discounts. You name it, we tried it. But even though our ortho tech was the best around, we couldn't shake the grim effect of recession on our falling conversion rate. Perhaps worst of all, I could tell my office manager was burning out. Many of you may be feeling that way now.

Yet the fragility (and panic) my team and I felt during that period of low conversion was the crucible out of which OrthoFi software was created and proven—the result of mixing Dave Ternan's leadership, Jeff Kozlowski's numeric genius, and insight from a handful of other industry-leading orthodontists. Once we implemented this technological edge, we didn't just survive—we thrived! Our leaky-bucket practice stopped losing patients and began filling up again. And once we'd amassed and analyzed the financial data from several billion dollars' worth of patients in our orthodontic-specific CRM system, we knew why.

The information provided us with data-enabled insights that showed us how to retool all our processes in a way that boosted patient conversions dramatically. These numbers revealed the best ways to stop leaks and convert pending patients into treatment starts, enabling us to develop an efficient and effective sales-and-revenue-cycle-management process for orthodontic offices that does the following:

- Provides a system that helps boost starts with patient-friendly payment flexibility while using office-friendly payment plans as leverage to stabilize cash flow and turbocharge practice growth.
- Allows the implementation of optimized systems for back-office collections so that doctors can have fun focusing on treating patients and driving growth in their business.
- Creates an end-to-end solution harnessing the power of the big-four business principles:

1. *Flexibility* drives growth.
2. *Leverage* maintains balance.
3. *Systems* create focus.
4. *Culture* rewards winning.

After implementing these principles in my own practice and teaming with industry experts to show hundreds of others how to do the same, I've found the resulting increase in SDS and overall conversions to be far better than I ever anticipated. Using this approach has produced an average SDS conversion of over 85 percent for six consecutive years and counting. My team and I have achieved the efficiency and profitability we could only dream about during the Detroit recession, but we're not stopping now, and you don't have to either. Our aim in sharing all the information and process improvements we've learned is twofold: we want to help other orthodontic offices grow in the midst of a rapidly changing industry environment and ensure orthodontic patients stay where they belong—being treated by highly skilled and integrity-driven orthodontists.

Takeaways for Pending Patients—The Leaky Bucket

- Flexibility gives more people access to orthodontic treatment and converts a higher number of pending patients by making orthodontics affordable.
- Leverage enables you to increase conversions by offering patients *intelligent* financial flexibility while balancing that flexibility with improved same-day cash flow from a higher SDC rate (ours is 85+ percent) you can track and measure.
- Systems using CRM software enable you to reconfigure and streamline your new patient acquisition process to optimize your conversion rate most effectively during in-person or virtual consult environments.
- Culture gets better with success, and good team morale drives higher SDS.

A SUCCESSFUL CONCLUSION

We started out talking about the good old days when we really didn't have any competition—a time when we had approximately nine thousand orthodontists caring for three-hundred-million-plus people across the United States. Unfortunately, that high patient-doctor ratio made our systems increasingly fragile. But it doesn't have to stay that way! In his book *Antifragile: Things That Gain from Disorder*, Nassim Nicholas Taleb promotes the useful idea that volatility and stressors can produce greater strength (not mere resilience)—a strength he terms *antifragility*. Just like bones bulk up from fighting gravity, a business's strength increases and becomes more "antifragile" from the impact of industry stressors. For the ortho industry, those stressors are the "low-cost" dentists and direct-to-consumer corporations disrupting industry norms and forcing the development of stronger, better processes. Such processes are built around data-driven analytics that shows what's most profitable for you and desirable to your patients. Outmoded orthodontic practices that refuse to offer flexible payment terms and scheduling, for example, or continue to use outdated technology are contributing to our industry's fragility and worsening the effect of disruption caused by DTC competitors.

With dental and ortho school tuition skyrocketing and student debt ballooning, a growing number of talented grads are struggling to make ends meet. This daunting situation is compounded by an orthodontic industry that has grown complacent from decades of almost zero meaningful competition. That reality and its consequences (i.e., perpetuating outdated and lazy business principles) have made the orthodontic industry ripe for disruption. These savvy industry disruptors have smart businesspeople at the helm, and they're winning against ortho specialists who require too many appointments and inflexible financing, trying to cover the big up-front lab fees associated with new ortho technology.

Orthodontists who do decide to invest in high-demand tech are getting stuck between the price pressure being applied by low-cost orthos or primary-care dentists and the higher up-front cost of popular technology. Like most doctors, you probably love clinical technology and customization, for example, and you know it's the future of the profession. But these technologies aren't getting less expensive. And you're undoubtedly feeling that using the best tech is making your job harder, stretching and squeezing your cash flow as you're forced to compete with the growing hordes of DTC and price-cutting competitors. You're also likely aware that people are flocking in droves to clinics that care nothing about them and to general dentists who take weekend courses, then undercut your prices and badmouth your office. Some consumers skip seeing a doctor altogether in response to industry disruptors'

> PEOPLE WANT BRACES THAT ARE QUICK, EASY, AND AFFORDABLE. YOUR CHALLENGE IS TO DO THAT WHILE ALSO PROVIDING THE SERVICE AND CLINICAL RESULTS THEY PROBABLY DON'T KNOW THEY WANT OR NEED.

savvy marketing techniques advertising maximum convenience and a much lower price for their "treatment."

The success of this marketing message conveys a valuable lesson you can put to use right away: people want braces that are quick, easy, and affordable. Your challenge is to do that while also providing the service and clinical results they probably don't know they want or need. To succeed with this medically responsible approach requires educating consumers about the essential value of your services (such as why they should care about correcting their bite) and helping them overcome any objections they may have to choose treatment with you. Since you have so many years of specialized training as an orthodontist, you deserve to treat orthodontic patients because you offer the best quality care—the kind of care your patients deserve. That's certainly not what your DTC and price-cutting competition are providing.

Orthodontists need to fight back with a dual, simultaneous approach. One part of this method requires doctors to use marketing to educate consumers about the medical superiority, safety, and outcome of their treatment. The second part calls for doctors to arm themselves with the newest business and sales strategies, using innovative tools and processes to actuate their practice growth. We realize asking doctors to focus on the business aspect of their offices may seem contrary to the clinical emphasis the majority of orthodontists really care about. But like it or not, competing for consumers' business by changing your own marketing and business practices is actually the best way to advocate for their medical interests. Standing your ground in what is now a very competitive industry will ensure that consumers/patients continue to be treated to the gold standard of clinical excellence. This is why gaining a key understanding of the business aspects of orthodontics has become integral to the future of the specialty.

Following the principles in this book means you don't have to start from scratch playing offense or devising a proven business strategy. We've shown you how to innovate quickly with a consult specific to the unique demographics and status of your practice's current processes. Once you adopt and implement the optimal strategies we've discussed, you'll be ready to compete more effectively in the new and rapidly changing orthodontic environment. Your practice, your patients, your team, and your community will thank you for it!

Printed in the USA
CPSIA information can be obtained
at www.ICGtesting.com
JSHW022333140824
68134JS00019B/1461

9 781642 256437